TEILHARD'S MYSTICISM OF KNOWING

TEILHARD'S MYSTICISM OF KNOWING

by Thomas M. King

THE SEABURY PRESS : NEW YORK

1981
The Seabury Press
815 Second Avenue
New York, N.Y. 10017

Library of Congress Cataloging in Publication Data
King, Thomas Mulvihill, 1929–
Teilhard's mysticism of knowing.
1. Teilhard de Chardin, Pierre—Knowledge,
Theory of. 2. Knowledge, Theory of. 3. God—
Knowableness. I. Title.
B2430.T374K5   121   80–25258
ISBN 0–8164–0491–7

CONTENTS

Preface

The writings of Teilhard de Chardin contain numerous cryptic passages that most of his commentators have overlooked. I found these passages to be suggestive and appealing long before I understood what they meant; I began collecting them and soon began to suspect that they outlined a careful unity of thought. In the present work I have brought the cryptic passages together in a unified statement that I hope will not prove cryptic at all. In the process I believe I have brought out a surprising and new dimension of this fascinating thinker. And I have also brought out a surprising and new dimension of myself!

In recent years there has been considerable interest in mysticism. But, for the most part, this interest has concerned various mysticisms of "unknowing." Teilhard was familiar with a form of this mysticism in his early years; but he questioned the experience until it "reversed" and he began to develop a mysticism of knowing—particularly as knowing relates to scientific discovery. As I began working on this study, a line from *The Phenomenon of Man* stood out in my mind: "Religion and science are the two conjugated faces or phases of one and the same complete act of knowledge." I set out to understand what Teilhard meant by a complete act of knowledge. I now believe the real significance of Teilhard is not that he might have reconciled truths of modern science with truths of Christian faith, nor that he was a Christian mystic with a considerable scientific achievement (several hundred published articles); rather, it is in Teilhard's exuberant claim that in the very act of scientifically achieving, he knew God. Teilhard began writing a theology of process and many of his readers came to see as he had seen; for when human knowledge is in process, God is found in the act of knowing.

To indicate in advance the line of thought developed in this study I would propose that the reader peruse a poem, "Everyman," written by

Edith Anne Stewart. The poem is found in C. H. Dodd's study of St. Paul: *The Meaning of Paul for Today.* Dodd is commenting on a difficult passage in St. Paul to the Romans. Paul speaks of all creation groaning in travail and longing for the revelation of the sons of God so that it might escape its bondage to decay. To explain the passage Dodd quotes "Everyman," claiming that it presents beautifully a thought akin to that of St. Paul:

> *All things search until they find*
> *God through the gateway of thy mind.*
>
> *Highest star and humblest clod*
> *Turn home through thee to God.*
>
> *When thou rejoicest in the rose*
> *Blissful from earth to heaven she goes;*
>
> *Upon thy bosom summer seas*
> *Escape from their captivities;*
>
> *Within thy sleep the sightless eyes*
> *Of night revisage Paradise:*
>
> *In thy soft awe yon mountain high*
> *To his creator draweth nigh;*
>
> *This lonely tarn reflecting thee,*
> *Returneth to eternity;*
>
> *And thus in thee the circuit vast*
> *Is rounded and complete at last,*
>
> *And at last, through thee revealed*
> *To God, what time and space concealed.*

The poem also presents a thought akin to the thought of Teilhard that will be presented in this study.

In writing this work I have taken into consideration all of the available writings of Teilhard. This includes his unpublished letters (about 2,000) at the Teilhard Foundation in Paris and his unpublished notebooks at the Jesuit residence at Chantilly. At Chantilly there are eleven copybooks that Teilhard filled with jottings, diagrams and many incomplete ideas. These all date from his return from China (1946) and contain little of biographical interest other than the date and place of each entry. At Chantilly there are also several notebooks relating to his own readings and a small book in which he wrote daily reflections on his prayer during his annual eight-day retreat. All of these present a striking picture of Teilhard's mind: active with new enthusiasms and hesitations in the final years of his life. I have photocopied the pages of his notebooks which seemed most significant for this study; these are available at the Woodstock Library at Georgetown University. I have had two helpful conversations with Mlle. Jeanne Mortier, Teilhard's friend and literary executrice; she steered me away from a false interpretation of Teilhard, for which I am grateful. The librarian at the Teilhard Foundation, the Jesuit Rector at Chantilly, and numerous others, kindly assisted me in bringing this work to completion.

List of Abbreviations

Works by Teilhard Cited in the Text

AE *Activation of Energy,* translated by Rene Hague. New York: Harvest Book, Harcourt Brace Jovanovich, 1963.

AM *The Appearance of Man,* translated by J.M. Cohen. New York: Harper & Row, 1965.

C *Christianity and Evolution,* translated by Rene Hague. New York: Harcourt Brace Jovanovich, A Harvest Book, 1971.

D *The Divine Milieu,* translator unidentified. New York and Evanston: Harper & Row, Harper Torchbooks, 1960.

F *The Future of Man,* translated by Norman Denny. New York and Evanston: Harper & Row, 1964.

HE *Human Energy,* translated by J.M. Cohen. New York: Harcourt Brace Jovanovich, A Harvest Book, 1969.

HM *The Heart of the Matter,* translated by Rene Hague. New York and London: Harcourt Brace Jovanovich, 1979.

HU *Hymn of the Universe,* translated by Gerald Vann, O.P. New York and Evanston: Harper and Row, Colophon Books, 1965.

J *Journal,* Tome I (cahiers 1–5) (26/Aug/1917–4/Jan/1919), texte integral publié par Nicole et Karl Schmitz-Moormann. Paris:

Fayard, 1975. J followed by a date refers to the unpublished notebooks from the last eight years of Teilhard's life. These are at the Jesuit residence at Chantilly, France.

Lf   *Lettres familières de Pierre Teilhard de Chardin, mon ami.* 1948–1955. Written to Pierre LeRoy. Paris: Le Centurion, 1976.

Li   *Lettres intimes.* Written to Auguste Valensin, Bruno de Solages & Henri de Lubac. Paris: Aubier-Montaigne, 1972.

LLZ   *Letters to Leontine Zanta,* translated by Bernard Wall. New York and Evanston: Harper & Row, 1969.

LT   *Letters from a Traveller,* translator not identified. New York and Evanston: Harper & Row, Harper Torchbooks, 1962.

LTF   *Letters to Two Friends,* 1926–1952, New York and Cleveland: World Publishing, Meridian Books, 1969.

MM   *The Making of a Mind,* translated by Rene Hague. New York: Harper and Row, 1965.

MPN   *Man's Place in Nature,* translated by Rene Hague. New York, Evanston, San Francisco, London: Harper and Row, Colophon Books, 1966.

P   *The Phenomenon of Man,* translated by Bernard Wall. New York, Hagerstown, San Francisco, London: Harper and Row, Colophon Books, 1959.

S   *Science and Christ,* translated by Rene Hague. New York and Evanston: Harper and Row, 1968.

T   *Toward the Future,* translated by Rene Hague. New York, London: Harcourt Brace Jovanovich, 1975.

UP   *Unpublished Letters,* followed by name and date, filed alphabetical- !y according to addressee at Teilhard Foundation in Paris; where several letters are to the same person they are filed chronologically.

V   *The Vision of the Past,* translated by J.M. Cohen. New York and Evanston: Harper and Row, 1966.

W   *Writings in Time of War,* translated by Rene Hague. New York and Evanston: Harper and Row, 1968.

Retreat Notes	At Teilhard's death notebooks and papers left in his room were sent to France and are now at the Jesuit residence in
Notebooks	Chantilly. These are mostly notations of ideas written in a personal shorthand; frequently the notations are incomplete
Journal	sentences connected by arrows etc.

Works by Other Authors Cited in the Text

Augustine, *The Confessions of St. Augustine,* translated by Rex Warner. New York: New American Library, 1963.

Cuénot, Claude, *Teilhard de Chardin, A Biographical Study,* translated by Vincent Colimore. London: Burns & Oates, 1965.

Darwin, Charles, *The Origin of Species.* Baltimore: Penguin Books, 1968.

DeLubac, Henri, *The Eternal Feminine,* translated by Rene Hague. London: Collins, 1971.

Dobzhansky, Theodosius, *The Biology of Ultimate Concern,* New York: The New American Library, 1968.

Dodd, C.H., *The Meaning of Paul for Today.* Cleveland and New York: Meridian Books, World Publishing, 1968.

Kierkegaard, Soren, *Fear and Trembling,* translated by Walter Lowrie. Princeton: Princeton University Press, 1941.

Lukas, Mary and Ellen, *Teilhard.* New York: Doubleday, 1977.

Sartre, Jean-Paul, *Baudelaire,* translated by Martin Turnell. New York: New Directions, 1967.

TEILHARD'S MYSTICISM OF KNOWING

Chapter One

SUNLIGHT IN THE FRAGMENTS OF A BROKEN MIRROR
The Paradox of Matter and Spirit

Teilhard writes that he was no more than six or seven years old when he began to feel himself drawn by matter—or rather, he corrects himself, by something gleaming at the *heart* of matter. He began collecting scraps of iron found around his country home at Sarcenat in central France: part of a plough, a hexagonal-headed bolt, the fragment of a shell. He would call these his idols and would withdraw secretly to contemplate his "God of iron." He chose iron because in his limited experience he found nothing "harder, heavier, tougher, more durable than this marvellous substance." Upon finding that iron rusts and that it can be scratched—that is, it is transient—he tells of falling into the depths of childish despair. Soon he began looking for alternatives that were "resistant, impervious to attack and hard." Years later he would find a most unlikely substitute: "the supreme happiness that I had formerly looked for in iron was to be found only in spirit" (HM, 18, 19, 28). It seems paradoxical to suggest that spirit is hard, tough, heavy and durable, and more paradoxical still to compare it to metal and cement! Teilhard would often acknowledge the paradox that was present; but this fundamental paradox would become the basis of both his life and thought: he devoted his life to geological research —while claiming he was bored with the past; he felt at home only when he was "immersed in an ocean of matter"—yet longed to escape "the material plane"; he spoke with enthusiasm for a world that was changing with increasing rapidity—while seeking only "the Great Stability."

3

The Cosmic Sense

Shortly after his childhood disappointment with iron, Teilhard turned his attention to crystals of amethyst and quartz. He would see much significance in this change for his fascination with iron was directed to numerous fragments, but in switching to rocks he found himself involved with the entire planet; he had awakened to "the Stuff of things" (HM,20). He tells of soon becoming incapable of appreciating anything lacking a universal dimension. He believed a similar sensitivity was found in all people and was at the basis of all thought: "Ultimately, our thought cannot comprehend anything but the Whole, nor, when it really comes to the point, can our dreams entertain anything but the Whole" (C,58). Teilhard would call this sense of the universal the Cosmic Sense, or he would call it the Sense of Earth or the Sense of Plenitude, or even the Sense of Man or the Christic Sense. The different terms are not simply identical; rather the Cosmic Sense is a "protean element." But whatever shape it assumes or whatever it is called, the Cosmic Sense works against the common experience of multiplicity. Thus, Teilhard would see it as the common basis of any mysticism.

When Teilhard looked back on his life he would judge the external events to be only superficial ripples on a deep inner current based on the Cosmic Sense. The Cosmic Sense led him to develop an early interest in rocks and he began to study geology. He had come from a pious family and was himself a pious child. Shortly before his eighteenth birthday he entered the Jesuits and began his studies for the Catholic priesthood. His interest in geology would continue, and while teaching physics at the Jesuit school in Cairo he did some original research in nearby fossil beds. He then went to England to study theology, he was ordained, and two years later was drafted into the French army to serve throughout the First World War. It was during his military service, while he was acting as a stretcher bearer and under constant fire, that he began keeping a journal of ideas and writing speculative letters to his friends. In April of 1916 he wrote the first in a long series of philosophical-religious essays. It is from this time onward that one can follow the developments in his thought.

Many of Teilhard's early essays were written in the trenches between battles, but they also alluded to a more universal conflict:

> All around us, it would seem, there is nothing but incurable division and innate hostility (W,205).

The cosmos itself, taken in its totality, breaks down into a vast agglomeration of individual self-centered particles whose paths cross and obstruct one another (W,124).

Almost without exception, they each follow their own road, freely and egocentrically. Has the curve of my life anything in common with the fate of the insect scurrying at my feet (W,169)?

The multitude of beings is an infliction hard to bear (W,122).

But these oppressive perceptions are suddenly relieved by one of a very different type: separate things are perceived as elements within a wider whole. Perhaps the new perception begins when a limpid sound arises out of the silence, or a trail of pure color shimmers in a glass, or a light glows in the depths of someone's eyes. Such fleeting perceptions seem to draw Teilhard out of himself and into a wider reality: "I melted away in it, lost in a strange yearning to attain some individuality vaster and simpler than mine—as though I had become pure light" (W,118). This new perception is the reverse of the first: now hostility and alienation melt away. The dust of opposing particles becomes diaphanous in the discovery "of a super-real unity diffused throughout the immensity of the world."

At first this unity seems only an ethereal glow that lights the interior of things; then it becomes more firm and real than the plurality it unites. He, Teilhard, seems to touch the Being of Things, a universal physical entity, the One Thing Necessary, the All in which one recognizes God or the shadow of God (C,60). And when the moment of elation is over one is left with "a certain taste, a certain drunkenness for real concrete Being" (Li,121).

In recounting the experience Teilhard would tell of passing beyond himself to become part of a vast, all-encompassing unity; the perception itself had acted "to break up" his individual autonomy. He would come to argue that one can know the world only "by being co-extensive with it," by "becoming to some degree one body with it" (C,61,100). The world itself, the "Whole," is active in the process of knowledge; it is said to "assert itself" or to "reveal itself"; there is a "manifestation of the stuff of things." But there is also an active role on the part of the observer: there is a "transformation" of this Stuff in the perception itself. The Whole is "effected," it is "actualized," so that each perceiver is said to be a "particular actualizing of the Whole" (W,293;C,61,100; see Li,106).

Corresponding to the Cosmic Sense, man has a cosmic passion that is the "only primordial, irrepressibly ebullient passion in the human heart"

(W, 121). Teilhard's Cosmic Sense and passion were so vivid that he was always puzzled when others were insensitive to what he was experiencing:

> how has psychology been able so consistently to ignore this fundamental vibration whose ring can be heard by every practiced ear at the basis, or rather at the summit, of every great emotion? Resonance to the All—the keynote of pure poetry and pure religion (P, 266).

For Teilhard the Cosmic Sense is a primordial and pre-intellectual intuition; it is a matter of immediate experience. Thus it is a psychic fact that cannot be denied or argued away (W, 293). Though one could argue that the Cosmic Sense is all a matter of temperament—much as some people are said to have a temperament or taste for music while others do not—Teilhard was unwilling to let it be so relativized. He would argue that the Cosmic Sense characterized the first man; it has grown and developed with man; it is essential to being human; and as man further develops, its presence will be increasingly felt. Teilhard would acknowledge that it is more or less evident in different individuals. The man who is wholly taken up with the day-to-day concerns of life can have only a fleeting awareness of this second phase of perception and of the aureole that surrounds all things. But "the mystic is *the man who is born to* give first place in his experience to that aureole" (W, 119).

Regardless of whether or not one acknowledges his Cosmic Sense, the affect it has on one's life is invariably religious. Even the most unbelieving scientist is said to be sustained in his research by a sense of worship, for his interest in studying the cosmos proceeds from the depths of his soul reaching out to the universe, that is, to the All he unknowingly seeks. For Teilhard, there is no profound poetry, no lyricism or sublimity in the arts that does not rest upon an evocation and a presentiment of the Whole. Philosophers from the pre-Socratics down through Spinoza and Hegel have testified to its presence and articulated its nature. Thus, over all their works there passes the breath of worship.

Every mystical system, whether it is Christian or pagan, is said to be fed by the Cosmic Sense as by a "never failing spring" (W, 182, 121). Whenever Teilhard gives a systematic account of his own spirituality, it is with the Cosmic Sense that he always begins (HM, 16, 197; C, 96; W, 18, 117, 290; D, 130). He recommends that others draw nourishment from this source to sustain their own prayer: one must "carefully foster in himself his feeling for, his perception of, his zest for the Omnipresence which haloes everything in nature" (W, 121). The Cosmic Sense resembles an aesthetic awareness, so one finds that the arts can further sharpen one's sensibilities: music and painting can help "cosmicize" the soul (MM, 97).

When people first awaken to the Cosmic Sense they are "like children opening their eyes for the first time." They do not know how to locate or accurately place the reality they perceive all about them. The Cosmic Sense can lead one to a sublime love of God, but it can also lead to many other things; "seers" have often floundered and wandered off in false directions. "In this state, a little vague, all mystics take birth whether they remain aesthetic (poetry, music . . .) or deviate into pantheism" (Li, 106;J, 204).[1] The Cosmic Sense is said to be the beginning of prayer—but it is only a beginning. When it first affirms itself in a person it is primordial and pre-intellectual. In itself it does not involve the intellect—and many mystics have left it that way. They have developed a mysticism of "unknowing" or a mysticism that can be itself only through a rejection of all rational thought. The achievement of Teilhard is that his Cosmic Sense came to include his scientific understanding of the cosmos as well as his Christian faith. The Cosmic Sense is "protean," but to be complete it must encounter one's critical faculties and nourish one's innate desire to know. It may be snuffed out in the process. But in the end, "happy the man who will not shrink from a passionate questioning of the Muses and Cybele concerning his God" (W, 119).

The Reversal: Matter to Form

Teilhard would often refer to a "reversal," a "complete about-turn," in his understanding of the cosmos. This reversal seems to have begun in 1909, but it is difficult to date with precision as it proceeded slowly over the course of many years. He would tell of "gradually" developing a different world view (AE, 377), or state that "gradually . . . under the pressure of facts, I witnessed a reversal of the values" (CE, 113; see HM, 61).[2]

Teilhard was twenty-seven years old when he went to England to begin his study of theology. He had long been sensitive to the cosmic All, responded to it with reverence, studied the rocks, maintained a carefully observant Catholic faith, and was confused. The Cosmic Sense had led him to look for a permanence beneath the evident transience of the world.

He felt drawn to the common base of all things as to an amorphous "ultra-matter" underlying the divisions and separations of form: "If I was to be All, I must be fused with all" (HM,24). At this time he could envision only the pantheism of fusion and dissolution—what he was later to call the banal and facile form of the pantheist mind. He felt he had come to a dead end.

Then at the right moment, the idea of evolution began to germinate within him like a seed. He did not know where it came from, but tells of reading Henri Bergson's *Creative Evolution* which provided fuel for a fire already consuming his mind and heart. Evolution began haunting his thoughts like a tune; it was not so much an abstract idea, but a living presence. The presence seemed to involve a total drift of the cosmos; he came to realize that the cosmos he had always sensed was a cosmos in process. He began to see the forests of Sussex charged with the very life that he had been seeking in the fossil past; it seemed as though a universal Being was suddenly going to take shape in nature. But now the universal Being was not "ultra-material," rather it was "ultra-living." This is the reversal of which he so often spoke. Now his fascination with the cosmic All would not lead him in pursuit of an "ultra-matter," but in pursuit of "ultra-life." The *Unum Necessarium,* the divine consistence, had to be identified differently: "I had experienced a complete reversal of my Sense of Plenitude, and since those days I have constantly searched and progressed in that new direction" (HM,26).

Teilhard wrote an imaginary account of this reversal in his first essay. After some hesitation and changes he called the essay, "Cosmic Life." By the title he wanted to affirm that life has developed as a function of the cosmos; the cosmos is alive. He tells of his reversal in a more or less imaginary passage that begins with a descent into matter:

> One day, I was looking out over the dreary expanse of the desert. As far as the eye could see, the purple steps of the uplands rose in series, towards horizons of exotic wildness . . . or, buried in a forest whose life-laden shadows seemed to seek to absorb me in their deep, warm, folds—on such occasions, maybe, I have been possessed by a great yearning to go and find, far from men and far from toil the place where dwell the vast forces that cradle us and possess us, where my over-tense activity might indefinitely become ever more relaxed (W,29).

Matter was calling him to surrender in worship. Matter has its appeal; it seems to be the great stability that underlies the changing patterns on its surface; it seems to be the primordial and indestructible essence from which everything emerges and to which everything returns. Desiring to unite with the All he relaxes and drifts "unresistingly to effortless enjoyment and Nirvana" (W,32). Nirvana means a snuffing out of consciousness, and this is what he begins to sense. He begins to avoid social contacts and conflicts (was it not the elements in conflict that had first disturbed him?). He is summoned away from consciousness to silent untrodden places. He is lulled from responsibility and work: "Mighty nature is at work for us . . . any interference on our part would be wasted labor." The whole experience is termed, "the godless crisis into which I was flung by my initiation into the cosmos" (W,60).

Then the evolution of life wakens him from his numbing dream. In the evolution of life, matter is seen to be moving away from dissolution. The living earth is involved in a process away from Nirvana towards increased consciousness. He makes a reversal, and, henceforth, the direction of life will be his guide:

> When every certainty is shaken and every utterance falters, when every principle appears doubtful, then there is only one ultimate belief on which we can base our rudderless interior life: the belief *that there is an absolute direction* of growth (W,31–32).

This would be his earliest account of the "reversal," it was written in April of 1916. But though it tells of changing from "ultra-matter" to "ultra-life," Teilhard would soon consider the reversal incomplete for he had still allowed some unity to matter itself ("through the matter that is common to them, all living beings are but one 'being' (W,23). In November of 1917 Teilhard continued his reversal by stripping matter of both unity and being. He corrected what he had previously written:

> (In writing "Cosmic Life") I saw beings as held together principally by matter, so that, while fused together in their physical basis, they proceeded to disengage and isolate themselves in their spiritual apexes. I am now looking at it from a diametrically opposite point of view (W,168).

In "Cosmic Life" he had argued that any two objects chosen at random would have a hidden identity as they would be made of the same "prime matter." He had even developed the thought in a series of images:

> Like knots spaced out along a cord, or like the folds into which a single curtain falls, or the eddies forming on one and the same surface, everything that moves and lives in the universe represents, in one particular aspect, the modifications of one and the same thing (W,21).

Thus, even in 1916 his "reversal" had been far from complete. In 1917 he would renounce what he had written a year and a half earlier and take what he would consider a "diametrically opposite point of view": there is *no* unity in matter. In terms of the above images, there would be no single cord (with knots), no single curtain (with folds), and no single surface (with eddies). Matter is not single, it is multiple, it is radical multiplicity, "total disunity," "pure Multiple," "Incomparable Multiple," "infinite multiplicity." If one looks away from the unity given it by *form,* the world would appear "cantilevered" (W,160). Now Teilhard argues that the fundamental unity of the cosmos does not come from the common *root* of all things in matter—matter is total disunity—now the unity of the cosmos is seen to proceed from some *formae cosmicae* "imposed on the Multiple by a breath from on high." For these cosmic forms would further be united in a single all-embracing Form, the Form of Christ.

The paradoxical results of the reversal are now evident: in claiming that the universe has a single Form one goes against what generally seems to be experienced: Matter (not form) seems to be what all things have in common, hence it seems to be what unites them, while the evident plurality of forms seems to divide the unity of matter into separate beings. Teilhard would often acknowledge that what he was saying was opposed to this common and instinctive way of thinking. He was able to come to the position himself only by passing through an intermediate stage, for any justification for his claim had to depend on a radical understanding of evolution. Thus: there is now an evident diversity of forms, but through the process of evolution the different forms are becoming increasingly inter-related. Teilhard would further argue that this process of inter-relating will finally result in a single unified organism extending throughout the universe, an organism with a single unified form. Presently this unified Form is only the *goal* towards which all things are moving—thus, in Aristotelian terms, this unity could better be seen as a single Final Cause rather than as a single Formal Cause. But, apart from this reservation, one could say that Teilhard is proposing a modified philosophy of hylomorphism, a hylomorphism that is extended through time. For Teilhard, there was in the beginning only the radical plurality of matter and there will be at the end only the perfect unity of Form. This perfect form will be the form of the universal Christ and it will give a final unity to the cosmos. Matter is not the principle of unity; of itself matter has no unity: "it is obviously impossible to accept the spurious hypothesis of a multiplicity that contains its own principle of unification" (W, 160). Perhaps an analogy could illustrate the difference between unity in matter and unity in form. One might imagine the pieces of a plastic jigsaw puzzle spread out over a table. These would represent the separate elements that seemingly constitute the world. These might be brought together in two ways: First, one might melt the pieces to form a single lump. This would give the pieces a certain quasi-unity as a mass of plastic. But each piece had been stamped with a design (the *formae cosmicae*), and in melting them together this design (form) would be lost. Instead of melting them together one could undertake a building process with the pieces so that small clusters of pieces are fit together (this would be the present state of the world and the clusters would be the present living organisms). Then from a consideration of the growth of the clusters up to the present time, one could even begin to anticipate the final outcome, were the building and fitting operation to be completed. The final design would be the *Forma Christi,* and it would be to achieve this final unified form that Teilhard would urge that humanity labor "to build the earth." This final unity would be a unity of structure.

In "Cosmic Life" Teilhard had actually spoken of three source of unity: First, he told of the unity all things have in sharing a common matter (W, 19ff); then, unity through sharing a common life (W, 23); and, finally, the unity of a common goal. Each unity offered a certain contact with God. This triad will appear frequently in Teilhard and is considered at length in Chapter Three. This sequence through three types of unity could best illustrate Teilhard's own development. Before he went to Sussex to begin studies in theology he was seeking the unity of fusion in a common matter. Then he became sensitive to the life all around him, the "ultra-living"; he read Bergson, saw unity in the whole life process, titled his first essay "Cosmic Life," and explained that it is "primarily through their all possessing life that they are welded into one" (W, 23). It was only in 1917 that he came to see the third type of unity, the unity of a final all-embracing Form. The same three phases are found in his sense for God. In February 1919, he would tell of:

> three successive stages which I *myself in real fact went through* before I arrived at a satisfactory solution of the interior problem of making one's way to God (W,294).

Since he considered his soul "irrevocably cosmic," each of these three stages is also cosmic. The first of the stages is identified as seeing the *Will* of God present "through all the influences to which we are subject." This does not immediately suggest a connection with matter; but in being "subject" to events beyond one's control one could be said to undergo the contingencies of matter. Accordingly, in Teilhard's early letters to his family he would often refer to unfortunate accidents as the Will of God. His Journal would also associate matter with the divine Will (J,28;see D,121).

The second stage was when Teilhard came to see "God's creative action" everywhere in the universe. This would parallel his sense for life, process, becoming, that he became aware of in Sussex and about which he wrote in "Cosmic Life": "I can feel God, touch Him, 'live' Him in the deep biological current that runs through my soul" (W,61). The third stage came only in 1917 when he "arrived at a conclusive explanation" of what he had long felt: God comes to us "under his *formal influx*." "What I was looking for was a flow of *formality* from God into myself." (W,296). Thus, it was finally in terms of the unity of matter with form that he came to believe his desire for union with God could be satisfied. All religious mysticism is aimed at union with God; thus, union is generally suggested by mystics in various inarticulate images. Teilhard is articulate in proposing hylomorphism, the union of matter with form, as the model for understanding man's union with God. But the "matter" that is united is not the single individual, rather it is all mankind:

> In truth Christ acts upon us *as a form,* and the *totality of souls* ready to receive it is the *matter* which interiorly (. . .) takes on form in him (W,266;see D,63).

Christ's influence on the world is "informing" (S,58), "quasi-formal" (V,304), "informative" (W,266), "information" (W,257,266). God is not present as "Matter of matters," but as "Form of forms" (W,275). As *"Forma mundi"* (W,274), he will give the world its "definitive form" (W,252), its "universal 'form' " (S,65). Developing the Greek word for form Teilhard would speak of "the morphogenic" influence of Grace (S,58), the "morphogenic power of the Good" (W,172), and the "morphogenic function of morality" (W,171). God gives form to human attitudes (D,47), and religion gives form to psychic energy (S,104). Shortly before his death Teilhard again envisioned God as "a sort of Formal Cause" of the world (C,239). Thus, in a variety of expressions and from 1917 till his death in 1955 Teilhard would see God's present influx and final union with the world in terms of Form.

Teilhard would often use three closely related words in ways that can be confusing: Form, Soul and Spirit. In the scholastic philosophy Teilhard studied for many years, the *Form* (essence or nature) of a living organism is the same as its *Soul.* Teilhard continues this scholastic usage: the matter of a living organism is drawn together and animated by its form, that is, by its soul. Teilhard would use the terms form and soul interchangeably (W,265,266,295,299; HM,227; V.247, etc. One use on W,295 would seem to be an exception). For Teilhard, *Spirit* has a different but related meaning. Spirit would be the totality of human souls gathered together and united by the Soul of Christ. Thus the Soul of Christ could be termed the "Soul of souls" (LLZ,87). Thus, Spirit would be the matter that is animated and united by the "Soul of souls," the "Form of forms." Perhaps an illustration could make more clear the two levels that are involved. In figure 1, F,G,H and I would be the elements of matter united by human soul, A. Then A,B,C,D and E would be different human souls which taken together would be Spirit, and would serve as the matter united by Christ, the "Soul of souls." Thus, A,B,C,D and E would be called "true matter," "spiritual matter," or Spirit (See W,166ff;J,229). The two levels involved could be further clarified by a comparison with the human body: each cell in a body could be seen as having a certain "soul" of its own; but on another level, all such "souls" taken together form a single body with a common soul—a Soul of souls, so to speak. For Teilhard the entire universe is seen as a vast trans-human body in process of formation, and individuals would be like the partially separable cells which comprise the great Being that is coming to be. Ultimately, the Soul of Christ, the *Forma Christi,* will be the universal Form which governs the entire organism.

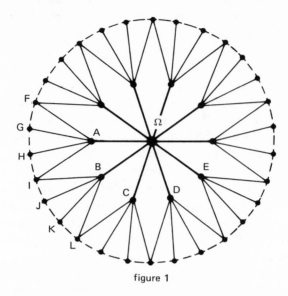

figure 1

Teilhard would speak of two fundamentally different types of pantheism that would be based on the two components, matter and form:

> in addition to *materialist pantheisms* (which look for the 'universal element' in a plastic or *informable principle of the world*) there is a whole category of *spiritual* pantheisms (which believe that this element may be found in a plasmatic or *informing* principle—vital or intellectual —of the universe) (W,273).

Thus, the reversal of which Teilhard often speaks could be seen as the change from a materialist to a spiritual pantheism. In the Cosmic Sense one is aware of being part of a single universal reality, but this reality could be identified as either a single unifying Matter or a single unifying Form. Those particularly sensitive to cosmic unity have generally envisioned a common matter as there does not seem to be any common form (the multiplicity of form seems to divide matter). This first impression is what must be reversed: manyness must be seen as applying to matter and unity to form. This reversal does not seem to have been considered by previous thinkers.

Teilhard would argue that it is only through the whole contemporary understanding of evolution that a spiritual pantheism can finally be coherently envisioned. Evolution reveals a gradual buildup of form throughout the ages; only recently could one envision a single all-pervasive Form at evolution's term. Thus, a spiritual pantheism had not been defensible; it needs "an informed observer" (W,24;S,31; MPN,74), "the informed eye" (see T,34,HM,60). This "informing" of the observer, or informing of the eye refers to the way one's knowledge influences one's vision and influences the Cosmic Sense. When Teilhard told of reaching a dead point in 1909 he added that what he needed was an "intervention." This came through his being *informed* about evolution, through reading Bergson who informed him of the cosmic extent of evolution, and through the formative power of grace that came through his faithfulness to prayer. Thus, the God that Teilhard claimed to find throughout the universe is *not* found directly in visible things, but "by a sort of reversal (*retournement*) of visible things—the notion and gesture of reversal must be discovered in the light of prayer" (UP, Mortier,Dec. 1939).

Teilhard would see St. Paul presenting a spiritual pantheism. But Teilhard believed many significant texts of St. Paul were overlooked because they could not be understood before the discovery of evolution. Teilhard found in St. Paul "the speculative model" of his own thought (see P,294). Thus St. Paul also "informed" his vision. St. Paul tells of all things being drawn into the Body of Christ and further urged men to build up Christ's body. Paul wrote of God's plan "to unite (to sum up) all things in Him (Christ)" so that finally at the end of the age when all is subject to Him "God may be all in all" (Eph. 1:10;I Cor.15:28).Thus Paul suggests a 'pantheism' at the end of time; he tells of Christ being all and in all, and sees the Body of Christ as "the fullness of Him who fills all in all" (Col.3:11;Eph.1:23).

There is another more or less pantheistic phrase of Paul that Teilhard would often quote: Paul sees all things created through Christ and "in Him all things hold together" (Col.1:17). Thus, Christ is seen as the *binding* force in the universe. Teilhard would quote this phrase in Latin: *in quo omnia constant* (D,122;MM,93;C, 71;AE,405). Starting from the Latin *constant,* and intensified by his own quest for unity, Teilhard would develop the term *Consistence* till it took on a richness of personal meaning: *"Consistence:* that has undoubtedly been for me the fundamental attribute of Being" (HM,18). Consistence is that which binds a substance so that it does not disintegrate into powder. Each scrap of iron he once collected was seen to have a great consistence, till it rusted and disintegrated. By virtue of his reversal Teilhard came to locate all consistence in Christ as the ultimate Soul of the World. In himself, Teilhard finds only an inconsistence; in his prayer he feels "totally without consistence"; he addresses Christ as his "sovereign Consistence" (W,123,128). By his reversal he came to see that "the consistence of the universe is 'Ahead in Spirit' and not 'Behind in Matter'" (UP,E.LeRoy,10/Aug/1929). He would urge others do the same: "We must reverse the crude view of things that would see consistence from below" (S,46). "The only consistence beings have comes to them from their *synthetic element*" (S,29). Thus, once again, it is form, the synthetic element, which gives consistence to the multiplicity of matter.

In terms of the contrast between the synthesizing (form) and the synthesized (matter) Teilhard had not yet clarified his thought even by November 1917 when he had corrected "Cosmic Life." Then he wrote: To be more is to be further united with more (*Plus esse = plus, eta pluribus uniri*), thus identifying *being* with the synthesiz*ed*. He would later reject this as the "materialist illusion," for it involves the bias that sees "the elements of analysis as 'more real' than the terms of synthesis" (C,105). In May of 1920, he would correct what he had written in 1917: "I would no longer say as before, 'Plus esse est plus, et a pluribus, un*iri*.'—but, 'Plus esse est plus et plura, un*ire*" (Li,60). Now, to be more is to unite more with more, it is not to *be* more united; greater being is identified with the active synthesizing element and not with what is synthesized. Then Teilhard would reflect that if being were not identified at all with the synthesized—there would *be* nothing to synthesize!

Teilhard began to encounter this basic dilemma of being-non-being in many ways: If matter is being drawn into being, where is it being drawn from? From non-being? Can non-being be (see W,95,163)? What Teilhard came upon is a set of dilemmas well known in the history of philosophy. There does not seem to be a simple solution.[3] Teilhard touched on the being of non-being in his first essay; there he referred to matter, the supremely dissociated multitude, as having "no existence . . . its essence . . . (is) to lie on the very verge of non-being" (W,95). Soon matter seems to have passed over the verge to become "positive non-being" located "at the opposite pole from being" (W,163–64). Thought is said to judge matter as "without legitimate existence" (C,57); later Teilhard speaks of it "to the extent it exists" (HE,102), only to conclude that it "no longer exists" (C,105). Teilhard seems to have innocently stumbled upon this whole set of philosophical dilemmas. He often alluded to them, would plead that he had no mind for metaphysical thinking, would put them aside only to take them up again.

But beyond any metaphysical dilemmas that bothered him, Teilhard was aware of a physical dilemma that arises from what scientists call entropy. He was probably aware of entropy for quite some time as he had taught physics at an elementary level in Cairo from 1905 to 1908. Also, in Bergson's book, *Creative Evolution,* that Teilhard found so influential, entropy was presented as a process opposing the movement of evolution. Entropy refers to the fact that in the course of every physical or chemical process there is a slight increase in the total *disorder* of the universe. Thus, physicists would see the universe as becoming increasingly disordered —that is, increasingly "amorphous." In evolution, forms of increasing complexity are building up while in entropy the complex forms are progressively breaking down. There are thus two fundamental currents in the universe. Teilhard would allude to the two on many occasions (F,50,81,91,188; HE,22,98;HM,84;C,109;T,114;S,95).

His earliest reference to them would seem to be a letter of July, 1915, wherein he sees them as two reverse perspectives that suggest his own reversal:

> Looked at in one way, nature is a drug, lulling us to sleep in the cradle of nirvana and all the ancient pantheism; in a more real way she is a penetrating summons to slow efforts . . . (MM,60).

Since evolution and entropy, build-up and decay, are opposing currents, any understanding of what the earth shall be in the end must indicate the final outcome of the opposition. Teilhard would envision a final separation, a split in the universe and an escape of spirit (T,47;AM,262ff). The psychic (the goal of evolution) will continue without matter (J,197); it will rise to divine union and the material remnant will sink back to chaos and "vanish in pure plurality" (HM,232). The need for the split would arise both from the reality of entropy and from Teilhard's own world-weariness: he would tell of a need to escape from space-time in order "to have the heart to press on" (AE,392). He would tell of the agony of feeling "imprisoned in the cosmic bubble" (HM,57), and explain to a friend, "I am impressed by the sort of sense of the smallness of the Earth . . . one begins to perceive the bars of the cage" (UP,E.Leroy,8/ Sept./1926).

This ultimate separation of matter and psyche is expressed many ways in the writings of Teilhard; sometimes it is indicated in vivid images: The earth will be "bleached to a uniform whiteness, like a great fossil"; then lest the Spirit that has matured remain "lashed to a corpse," the Spirit will depart (HM,189–90). "Spirit is the extract of the universe, like a precious metal" (J,220). The separation is often expressed abstractly: There will be "a liberation from the material plane of history and elevation in God" (HE,47). Mankind as a whole will "abandon its organo-planetary foothold"; Spirit will become detached "from its material matrix" at a "critical point simultaneously of emergence and emersion, of maturation and escape" (P,288). There will be released "in a free state, a thinking without a brain. The escape of some part of the *Weltstoff* from Entropy" (AM,264). The separation is also expressed as an arrow that rises and divides on a set of Cartesian coordinates; the drawing (figure 2) is found many times in his late Journals and appears twice in his published works (AE,335;AM,216). The drawing shows that for some time the psychic and the physical build up together. This refers to the way that as physical organisms developed in the course of evolution, their consciousness also increased. But at a critical point the two separate and go their different ways. This then is the split that results in "a thinking without a brain." The brain will have entropized but the consciousness will continue its rise into unity. This would be Teilhard's way of speaking of the death of an individual but even more so of the physical death of Mankind.

For several years Teilhard wrestled with the complexity found in any system that would speak of the eventual separation of the soul from matter: the soul of man is said to be the unifying principle of the matter it animates, but if the matter is removed there would be nothing left to unify and hence no principle of union. In terms of a geometrical image the soul can be seen as the center of a circle, but if the circle is taken away there is no longer a center. In February of 1917 Teilhard hesitatingly proposed a solution: during one's life something of the material world became spiritualized into the soul; this is what the soul would continue to unify after death.[4]

He would later develop this suggestion to explain that in *becoming known* the essence of the material world is entering into the soul of the knower. So he would speak of the world being found within our soul

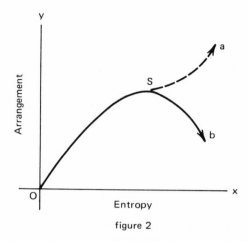

figure 2

(F,17), or see "the essence and the totality of a universe" being slowly deposited within man (P,180), or say that "the universe is concentrating itself in thought" (HE,98). Finally, when all that is of value in the material world has "passed into the souls of men," souls will separate from their material base (D,110). It is in this context that Teilhard would envision Spirit becoming "filled with the spoils of matter" (LT,151), or being "clothed in the spoils of matter" (J,229). In the end it would seem that the only way that matter enters into the final divine union would be in the souls of individual people, that is, by entering into the memories of those people. Thus the consummation of physical things is "bound up with the explicit perception we make of them" (P,249). He would quote with approval Charles de Bouvelles to the effect that all things strive to become thought. The material world can reach its final equilibrium only in becoming thought (T,165). Since the physical world would reach its eternal consummation only by entering human consciousness, Teilhard would press the value of scientific research; unless the physical is known by man its treasures will be irretrievably lost.

To sum up Teilhard's reversal: it began in 1909 when he was studying theology in England, but its full significance took more than a decade to realize. The reversal involved the "decrowning of matter" (J,227); it was "dethroned by Spirit" (J,205); it was progressively stripped of Unity, Being and Consistence; thus, Teilhard writes of the "annexation of the attributes that most attracted me in matter" (HM,206). Matter (as it is generally understood) is allowed to sink into nothingness, while Spirit (containing the spoils of matter) will one day break free of its material matrix and be eternalized as Christ's mystical Body. During this ten-year period of change Teilhard reversed his "instinctive predilection for matter" (HM,198). What once had fascinated him in matter was gradually seen to be no more than a reflection or an echo of the rising of Spirit. Thus it is Spirit that provides him with the happiness once found in iron. But in the process Spirit is "filled with the spoils of matter"; that is, Spirit is said to be durable and solid; it has become a "solid block," it is "like some molten alloy . . . in process of solidification" (HM,183–84), like "a precious metal"; it is seen as "sparkling drops of pure metal . . . forming on the inner surface of things" (HU,48); it is said to have "concrete meaning," or referred to as "the cement is setting" (HM, 35,185). These paradoxical images of Spirit developed out of Teilhard's progressive understanding of the reversal he had experienced in Sussex. He had come to see that the stability generally assumed to be in matter was only an appearance in which one more or less mistakenly incarnates his dreams of the divine (MM,62). To correct this mistaken "incarnation" Teilhard had to develop a new and paradoxical way of thinking, speaking and perceiving. Physics would provide him with the vocabulary, the "archetypes," by which he would speak of God (HM,23). Teilhard would write theology in terms of weight, density, pressure, energy, force and radiation. He did not stumble into this unaccustomed way of speaking: by a conscious decision he resolved to take the attributes given to the physical world and "acclimatize" them in God (J,225).

Paradoxes of a Reversed World

Teilhard speaks of the "curiously seductive power" that gravity exerted on his young mind. Gravity was seen as a universal force drawing all matter together; thus it seemed to be the binding element that would give *consistence* to the Whole. So Teilhard would recall, "I ingenuously promised myself, at the age of twenty-two, that I would one day dedicate myself to unlocking" the secret of gravity (HM,23). But before he got around to acting on this dedication, his whole sense for matter underwent its reversal. Now his fascination for gravity would become a fascination for the attractive force drawing evolving life into ever more complex structures. He began seeking:

that as yet undiscovered and unnamed power which forces Matter (as it concentrates under pressure) to arrange itself in ever larger molecules, differentiated and organic in structure (HM,33).

Gravity would now serve as the image to explain this psychic drawing force. The pull of gravity downwards would be seen as "merely the reverse or shadow of that which really moves nature" (P,265). This upward "gravity" is not a gentle drift towards rest, but rather a "fundamental maelstrom," an "irresistible Vortex," spinning matter into ever more complex arrangements (HM,33,34).

Teilhard even planned to write an essay titled "The Physics of Spirit"; an essay that would manifest his reversal by showing "the world of present-day science exactly reversed"; things would be shown to "fall laboriously" upwards (Li,183). He never wrote this essay, but throughout his writings there is the sense of matter being drawn into the future. There is a "fundamental tide inherent in Matter" that rises to increased structure and consciousness. Matter rises into consciousness because the future exerts an attractive power so that the world "falls forward in the direction of Spirit," "with all its weight it falls forward in equlibrium" (HM,28,35). A loving and attracting Presence is seen to act as a Final Cause drawing all things forward into union.

It was Teilhard's instinctive predilection for matter that led him to study rocks and the geological past. But with his reversal he found "the balance of the world reversed from what lies behind to what lies ahead" (HM,38). He then directed his attention towards the future. He continued to explore the past, but frequently found that his work in geology was at odds with his true interest: "Today what counts for me . . . is the future of things; whereas here I am plunged into the past" (LT,81). And, "I am a pilgrim of the future on my way back from a journey made entirely in the past" (LT,101). At times he still spoke of his fieldwork with enthusiasm, but he would also tell of "a certain disillusion" with the work for, "the exploration of the past . . . in itself is empty and deceiving." "It is the future which is fascinating" (Li,307). The "luminous shades" that once drew him to study the past were judged to be "no more than a mirage," only a reflection of what is ahead (V,187).

Nature is seen to show an "almost heart-rending effort towards light and consciousness" (MM,62). In Christ all things will find their future consummation and their true unity: "the whole itself holds together only through its future fulfillment" (C,71); it is "cantilevered on," "supported solely by" the future (AE,239;HE,45). Since things hold together through their future unity in Christ, the *outcome* of the process is assured. Again, the common way of thinking is reversed: Instinctively men tend to regard the past as fixed and assured while the future looms hazardous and uncertain. But if one believes that Christ is guiding life to its future in himself, then the entire situation is reversed and the future becomes stable and defined. It is "the future and not the past that becomes the direction in which being attains solidity, density and stability" (W,169–70). But unwilling to believe, men cling to "the apparently more solid framework of what has already been acquired and of the past" (W,226). The past is only apparently definitive and the future only apparently subject to chance; this appearance must be reversed:

> The chaotic appearance of the future is due to our seeing the development of the universe "the wrong way" or "from the underside." We are looking at a tapestry from the back, or playing a piece of music backwards. If we are to appreciate the harmony of events, they must be looked at "in descending order"; we must, that is, start from the results—for to produce these results events were set in motion (W,240, translation amended).

If we believe that Christ is the final term of the universe, then the outcome of the process is not in doubt. In urging that we must "start from the results" in order to understand the earlier parts of the process, Teilhard is telling of the methodology he used in many of his own essays: *The Phenomenon of Man* begins with a long consideration of the original matter of the universe; but the nature of this original matter is explained in terms of what it *must have been* in order to *result* in the world of today. Then, in the final section of the book, Teilhard interprets present-day social phenomena in terms of the society and fulfillment he envisions for the future. History is seen in reverse order, for it is only in this way that it can be understood (D,125). It can be understood in the reverse of the way it is lived.

If we believe that Christ is the terminus of the universe calling all things to advance into himself, our whole perspective is changed. Everything is illuminated. Chance is seen to be order, each success incorruptible; and we can advance in confidence. But if we do not believe there will be such a future, the sky remains dark, the waters shifting, zest for action is paralyzed, "And we may hear the voice of the Master, faced with our bungled lives: 'O men of little faith, why have you doubted?' " (D,136).

Nature *seems* to advance with little consideration for what the outcome will be. But man partially stands apart from Nature and questions where all his effort is leading. For a reflective being to act he or she must first believe that there will be an outcome that will justify the act; there must be a suitable goal, and thus people need "the expectation of a supreme Summit of consciousness" (HM,97). Teilhard would interpret the Existentialism popular in the late 1940s as an expression of fear coming out of a sense of a meaningless universe. As man becomes increasingly reflective, the question of goals becomes increasingly insistent. The existential dread is really a cosmic *angst* by which it becomes increasingly difficult for one to act (AE,184). Teilhard read Sartre's *Nausea* and copied out several passages wherein the absurdity of the world paralyzes all activity ("I know very well I do not want to do anything," etc. —Notebook dated 1945). But if instead of being lost in a meaningless process one sees a loving God as the consummation to which all things are advancing, existential dread is *reversed* into existential love" (AE,194). One's zest for action is increased and through such action the universe itself advances towards its goal. Teilhard knew existential anxiety and its attendant paralysis. He claimed he would not be able to lift a finger unless he believed there would be a suitable and eternal outcome to it all. He would argue that only a religious goal can motivate the person who reflects (the aetheist Sartre would write, "For a thoughtful person every enterprise is absurd." Sartre, *Baudelaire,* 31). Thus true religion is not an "opium of the people" drawing them apart from the human task, rather it is the summons to action that enables reflective life to move the great work of evolution to its completion. Teilhard would suggest that religious creeds be evaluated by their ability to stimulate action. The creed that presents a loving God as the future goal of the universe will be the creed of tomorrow, the "Religion of Evolution" (HM,97;AE,390). Teilhard found this creed in the Pauline vision of Christ uniting in himself all creation; he "in whom all things hold together."

Teilhard's reversal also led him to a somewhat paradoxical understanding of love: virginity is the highest form of love, while purity involves a "passion of extraordinary richness and intensity" (W, 108). The common assumption is reversed, for if one were to inquire how the unity of lovers comes about, most people would "instinctively give the easy answer 'through matter'." Lovers feel themselves driven by passion to melt into each other and seek this unity through ever more material means. These increasingly material expressions of love soon bring surfeit and disgust; the more lovers try to meet in this way, the more they drift apart. They fail because matter is not the principle of union, it only appears that way. In embracing matter, the "fragile links" of spirit are broken. Lovers can truly come together only in the depths of their spirit (W, 103, 170–71). Unaware of this or unwilling to see it lovers cast themselves into an "abyss of selfish pleasure . . . deceived by a reflection or by an echo" (HU, 70). When a man seeks a woman only for pleasure, he pursues a "deceptive image," an "inverted semblance," of what a woman truly is; a false image lures him into matter. Eventually he will find that he has been reduced to dust and dust is all that he embraces. He will find only "the lower multiple (that reversed image of God)" (W, 196). Thus with human lovers, true consistence or binding power is not found by their reverting to their origins in matter, but only by striving towards the future in Christ "in whom all things hold together."

The most evident paradox that followed from Teilhard's reversal concerns his sense for the durable, the unalterable, the stable. As a child Teilhard had reverenced scraps of metal because of their apparent stability. But as each scrap "showed itself to be unstable and perishable" he directed his attention to the totality of matter. Teilhard would judge such a tendency to be common; people have "an instinctive tendency" to look to formless matter wherein they can find a "primordial stability" (AE, 377). Scientists in particular are given to this tendency, for entropy has shown that the structures of the universe are increasingly breaking down. Thus it is "on the *elementary* side—that is, towards matter infinitely diluted —that physics and biology look to find the eternal and the Great Stability" (P, 268). By his reversal Teilhard came to believe that the final stability is not to be found in matter but rather at the terminus of the building processes of life:

> The world does not hold together 'from below' but 'from above'.
> Nothing is seemingly more unstable than the syntheses gradually

effected by life. And yet it is in the direction of these fragile constructions that evolution advances, never to fall back (C,113).

The living forms appear fragile, but they are being drawn to a final form that will not perish because it is of God. Thus, one comes to see:

> the paradoxical solidity of what is most fragile. Contrary to the appearances still admitted by physics, the Great Stability is not at the bottom in the infra-elementary sphere, but at the top in the ultra-synthetic sphere (P,271).

At the beginning of this chapter Teilhard was seen to speak of a double perception: First, there was the common perception by which things are seen to be entirely separate, locked-in on themselves, and going their separate ways; this gave rise to distress. This perception was relieved by a second perception in which all things were seen to pass out of themselves and become parts of a wider whole. Corresponding to these perceptions Teilhard would see everything in the universe having two properties, immanence and transience. That is, everything is "at the same time itself and something else" (W,167). This "being-other-than-itself" is what gives each being an instability, but it is also that which enables beings to interact, to pass out of themselves and thus be elements in a wider whole. The two properties (immanence and transience) could be illustrated by considering one cell within a multi-celled organism; it is both itself (immanent) and part of a wider whole (transient). Teilhard would see the same two properties in every element in the universe and in terms of them his reversal would involve a shift in interest from what an element is in itself to what it is beyond itself, from the immanence by which iron is purely itself to the transience by which it could rust and become other. Thus, Teilhard would write that an element is constituted "by that which is commonly called the 'beyond it' ('*l'en dehors d'elle*') rather than by its center" (J,185). Teilhard's concern shifted from the apparent stability of iron to the real instability of all things. The instability or transience of things is what enables them to pass out of themselves to share in a common spirit. It is upon this spirit, that is, the communality of all things, that God will ultimately impose his eternal stability. The transience that we now experience is that of a passage: all things are passing out of their separate immanence and into an all-embracing immanence that is coming to be:

> *The sum* of the universe's *transience* will continue to increase until the time when it attains the value of an immanence that will embrace all things in a sort of common soul (W,167–68). The most absolute form of immanence that we know is the Spirit (J,217).

In the process of evolution the elements increasingly pass out of themselves to become part of a growing common movement of life; in the process of entropy the elements increasingly turn in on themselves to become increasingly isolated. Teilhard plays upon the words and says that the universe "lends itself to *e*volution (life) and *in*volution (entropy)" (HE,23; parentheses in text). In evolution the elements become increasingly inter-organized (animals within an eco-system, people within humanity, etc.) and this increasing inter-organization is the rising spirit of the earth. The formation of this Spirit is the "goal towards which nature's age-long labors are directed" (W,137), as well as the goal of man's reflective labor (P,253). *In itself* Spirit can be described as "maximum instability" and "the latest and most fragile product of the Cosmos," for that is how it is perceived; but by the reversal it is seen as "the indestructible part" of the cosmos for it is what will be raised by God "to final union" (J,217,227;HE,41,179). Thus Teilhard insists, "I do not confer any 'divine stability' on the natural order. I would rather say the natural order is characterized by a radical instability in Christ"; thus Christ "physically stabilizes" the radical instability of Spirit (Li,35;J,32). Spirit is the matter ("this paradoxical conclusion, 'true' matter is Spirit" J,229;W,166–168) on which God bestows the stabilizing form of his Christ. Man has a role to play in the process in that by his work he further unifies the earth, that is, he increases the transience or communality of things; this is "the natural liberation of Spirit by work." This first phase is followed by "its divinization by grace" (W,142). Thus, there are two phases in the total process: one is natural and the other is supernatural:

> 'Everything in the Cosmos is for Spirit'; that, in natural terms, is
> the verse,
> 'Everything, in Spirit, is for Christ'; and that, in supernatural terms, is
> the verse of the Gospel that our modern World needs (HM,216).
> All well-ordered activity here below is directed *towards Spirit,* and Spirit
> *towards Christ* (W,300).

Teilhard would see his own life as a quest for the durable, but by his reversal he came to seek the durable in that which appears most fragile, he came to seek the Great Stability in that which appears most instable, he came to seek the Great Immanence where matter appears most transient. Teilhard seems to delight in the "paradoxical nature" of what he is saying as he claims that "the most real, most absolute is the most hazardous, the most contingent" (J,226); and he judges transience to be the foundation "of the stability of being," the "growing trace of unification *in fieri*" (J,228). After his wartime essays Teilhard did not make abundant use of the word transient; instead he spoke of Becoming, Movement, Process and Action. Forty years after his original reversal he was still trying to articulate and name again what he had discovered years before: "The essence of matter, that which I was seeking in the rocks and woods of Sussex, is the Cosmic Flux of Convergence" (J,8/Aug/52); it is the "universal Flux both unifying and irreversifying" (HM,87). Flux became a favorite word in the last years of his Journal. Such was the reversal that began among the rocks of Sussex; a shift from the apparent stability of things in themselves, to the real instability of things passing beyond themselves in a Cosmic Flux of Convergence. Everything was seen to be in movement; the cosmos is a vast cosmogenesis. Even the rocks, whose "stability" he so esteemed as a boy, are only moments of a passage:

> The mineral world is a much more supple and mobile world than could be imagined by the science of the ancients . . . there occurs in the most solid rocks, as we now know, perpetual transformations of mineral species (P,69). Once upon a time everything seemed fixed and solid. Now everything in the universe has begun to slide under our feet: mountains, continents, life, and even matter itself (V,238).

We have to surrender "the illusion of immobility," for science is showing that "all inertia resolves itself into movements of incredible rapidity" (V,143,239). And science will make further progress only "by peeling away, one after another, all the coverings of apparent stability in the world" (F,65). The stability that we think we see in nature is only an appearance wherein we mistakenly incarnate our dream of God (MM,62). Man himself is "seen to be the most mobile thing in the world"; while the question of man's place in nature "has become Man's movement in nature" (AE,327,313).

Process becomes the basis of Teilhard's ethic: the individual has no right to remain inactive (F,202). The threat of war hangs over the world because people have not sufficiently purified themselves of the demon of immobility (F,159). The real conflict is between "fixists" and "mobilists," but "mobility" is the only value worth dying for. The battlefield itself brings one "to the level of the world in movement, in activity, in progress" (J,222). Man makes a fundamental error when he believes that the Feminine is immobile—the feminine is really rising spirit (J,298). Socialization brings about "the acceleration of life" (J,2/July/51). Property has evaporated "into something fluid," and the world of human thought is "more fluid than any liquid" (V,164). Teilhard envisioned ever more rapid systems of transportation and communication, with growth in international trade ("accumulated riches will regain motion . . . material energy will circulate" [HE,38]. The significance of all the corresponding technological development is that it brings about in man the "acceleration of the cerebral faculty of thought" (AE,353). Teilhard's ethic of action is aimed at increasing the communality of things and thus the communality of Man; that is, he is trying to build up the Spirit, increase the transience and draw all things out of themselves into the rising Flux of Convergence. For Christ bestows his presence on a "universe in a state of accelerated evolution" (J,8/Jan/55).

Movement is also the basis of the spirituality of Teilhard. He would seek the Lord by " 'communicating' with the Becoming of things"; he regarded such communion as "the formula" for his entire life (LT,255, 283). Spirit itself is only a process ("the true name for 'spirit' is 'spiritualization' " [HE,96]. Nothing else in the world is as active as purity and prayer, while the mystic is characterized by "insatiable activity" (W,138). The mystic must pass out of himself into the converging Flux and must become transient for, "man has no value save for that part of himself which passes into the universe" (HU,65). Burned across the forehead of the seer is the motto: "Nothing is precious save what is yourself in others and others in yourself" (HU,62). Thus Teilhard would tell of his own yearning to pass into something beyond himself:

> I find the need of finding in me or around me something more stable and more consistent than myself wherein to transpose myself. Instinctively I try to reattach myself to the element that is material, or dynamic, or a collection of beings, that is to say, to all that which is not essentially individual (J,196).

During his stay in Sussex (1908–1912) Teilhard felt drawn out of his individual immanence to become part of the vast process of life. Soon he was working with other scientists in common research. Then he was drafted into the French army where the common movement of large numbers of troops made him feel part of a vast biological undertaking. Individuals were urged to sacrifice themselves for France and the life of mankind. Teilhard thrilled at the common dedication of the soldiers and sensed himself living a wider life. This process of transience or passing out of oneself is found in "the consecration of the individual to universal causes," and expresses the idea that "the most logical term [of the process of passing out of oneself] in the end is death" (J,222). Thus, the individual gains value through the sacrifice of his own individual immanence, but in the sacrifice he finds another Immanence. In coming to realize this Teilhard discovered again the paradox at the heart of Christianity: one must lose oneself in order to find oneself. To gain an ultimate stability in God, one must first make the act of faith wherein one passes out of oneself, that is, each person must become completely transient: "there must be felt an absolute passing through (transience) into Omega, that is, not an iota of viscosity, of sticking to things (viscosity)" (J,8/Oct. /21;deLub,*EtFem.*215).

When Teilhard finished his military service, he returned to the Sorbonne and completed his doctoral work in geology. Soon he left France to begin the first of many geological expeditions in China. Through travels in China, Java, India, Africa, Europe and the United States his thought continued to clarify, but it did not fundamentally change. He always believed his thought was developing, so much so that late in life he was "astonished" to read what he had written twenty years before and find he still presented the same vision (HM,47–48). His ideas had become more complete, their emphasis had altered, but after his wartime essays they remained the same.[5]

Though Teilhard often told of his reversal and how his interest had turned from matter and the past towards spirit and the future, he continued to be stimulated by his field-work in geology and truly felt at home when immersed in an ocean of matter (HM,20). Matter enabled him "to communicate with the Becoming." Matter continued to present itself as durable, stable and consistent. But because of the "reversal" Teilhard had come to see that matter does not really possess these properties, it only reflects back what is really on high. Scientists who do not acknowledge this truth have adopted a faulty perspective wherein they "turn their backs on the rising sun" (HE,174). Mystics with the same perspective seek to dissolve in matter, but they are only plunging into a well "in order to grasp the reflection of the sun" (C,124). Lovers with this erroneous perspective become selfish pleasure seekers in sex for they "are deceived by a reflection" (HU,70). The basis of all these errors is in the nature of matter—that fundamental paradox that has run through the history of philosophy: in itself matter has no real being, it is only the *reflector* of Being it does not possess; in itself matter has no real unity, it is only the *reflector* of a unity it does not possess; in itself matter is only "a mirror of shining particles" (see J,13/Dec/53).

At the age of six or seven Teilhard had become aware of something gleaming at the heart of matter. Soon he awakened to the Cosmic Sense. Others before him had known this sense, only to spend their days in the pursuit of a reflection. Teilhard undertook a "passionate questioning of the Muses" till a *reversal* occurred at the surface of multiplicity and he realized that the fascinating gleam was "like sunlight in the fragments of a broken mirror" (D,114). Matter is a mirror that *reverses* the direction of light. Matter is the great Paradox of Being; matter would lend paradox to Teilhard's life. Following the discovery and reversal Teilhard would commit himself anew to the study of geology; but he would seek to know only the Sun reflecting over the rocks. He knew that the radiance he saw in matter and the past were only reflections of what was above and ahead, but by studying the radiance in the rocks he would learn of the reflected God.

Sometimes Teilhard is a lyrical poet speaking in praise of matter; sometimes Teilhard is an idealist philosopher speaking of the triumph of mind. The difference is found in the great paradox: matter is the non-being that *is;* it only reflects. Thus, when we look into the depths of matter, we find that our regard plunges into "the infinite that *lies behind us*" (HM,225). Stability and consistence are reflected throughout the earth, but they are only found "behind us" where Christ bestows them on the rising Flux of Spirit. Behind us spirit is being rendered eternal, hard, firm and durable; the cement is setting; the molten alloy of spirit is in process of solidification.

Chapter Two

UNITY DIFFERENTIATES
The Consistence of Life and Truth

W hen matter presented itself as a temptation, it offered Teilhard a simple message: "everything in the universe is uniformly true," therefore let yourself be absorbed into matter "without distinction." Teilhard told of drifting in this direction—towards "a lack of thought"—but he was saved by a faith in life. Life rejects the amorphousness of matter; it makes distinctions and increasingly differentiates its elements. Thus, the movement of life serves as the guide for Teilhard's inner life, his thought. Life does not define dogmas, but it does indicate the direction in which one can "grow greater in the truth." Life and Truth or Life and Thought are often paired in the writings of Teilhard (W,140,301,231;MM,96, 149;AE,137;T,85;J,95,196). They are paired because the process of Truth in the mind is a continuation of the process of Life in the world.

Truth as Direction of Life
Teilhard frequently alludes to the "atomic" or granular character of the universe. That is, at all known levels of the universe we find it composed of more or less separable units or "grains": there are stars, atoms, molecules, cells, people, etc. Teilhard suggests that an atom would continue to break down into subatomic and sub-subatomic particles as long as one would continue dividing it in "an unending state of disintegration as it goes downward" (P,41). Sometimes the particles are gathered together in aggregations (a pile of sand, a galaxy of stars); sometimes they are linked together to form a crystal. But in both the aggregation and the crystal Teilhard sees only an external unity that is of no great interest. The number of molecules or particles brought together to form the crystal can be increased indefinitely to form a crystal of

unlimited size. In further adding molecules the original crystal is not modified, so Teilhard would argue there is no intrinsic bond. A very different type of bonding is found in the living cell: here each element is affected by all the others and by the whole of which it is a part. Thus, a cell appears limited in its contours (MPN,20). A crystal builds up through indefinitely repeating the same molecular pattern; while life builds up unities by structures ever more complex and intricately related. It is to this "center to center" bonding of "complexity"—a characteristic of all the living—that Teilhard directs his attention. For bonding power, that is, "Consistence," is what Teilhard always regarded as "the fundamental attribute of Being" (HM,18).

At some moment billions of years ago inert elements came together and formed the first living cell, "a cell is born." All of the separate elements were there before the cell appeared, but the unity itself was new. And this unity was more than the sum of its parts. In forming the cell the elements have not lost their original character to "become blurred and confused together." Rather, that which is distinctive about every one of the elements is accentuated, "their own nature is reinforced" (AE,116). "True unity does not fuse the elements it brings together," rather, "by mutual fertilization" it renews them (HE,63), or as Teilhard would often repeat, "Unity differentiates" (HE,63,67,83,144,152;AE,116;AM,212,269; C, 117;F,55;V,208;HM,141).

The living unity "super-differentiates" the elements that it unites (HE,42). This is again why the movement of life is the reverse of the movement to matter. Matter suggests a unity (one that is only apparent) in which all distinction is lost. But the living cell has a unity wherein the particular quality of each element—its form—is further intensified. The living organism does not dissolve the specific character of its elements, it needs this character, it accentuates it, and draws it into a more complex whole.

When the first cell was formed, the process of unification did not stop. The cell continued to reach beyond itself (transience) to find new elements and incorporate them into its unity. To describe this process Teilhard would use the word "groping." The cell gropes or feels beyond itself for what it can use. But Teilhard would also apply "groping" to the whole of life as it extends through the ages: Life is groping, it "can advance only by endlessly feeling its way" (T,170). Many followers of Darwin have argued that life advances only because some *chance* mutations are better able to survive than others. Teilhard's word, "groping," acknowledges an extensive dependence on chance, but it also affirms that life has a direction, an orientation, a preference. Groping is "directed chance" (P,110). Thus, life has had a finality from the beginning; it prefers increased life. Throughout its process it takes advantage of what it chances to find and puts it to its own use. But something can be advantageous only if there is a direction. Groping is a "combination of the play of chance (which is physical) and that of finality (which is psychic)" (AE,124; parenth. in text).[1]

Many biologists are reluctant to acknowledge any finality in evolution, but Teilhard would urge that when one acknowledges a simple finality, all the details of evolution are mutually clarified and rendered intelligible. Thus, he recognizes that random events largely determine the path life has followed and the forms it has assumed, but beyond these he would claim there was a direction present from the beginning. This direction will become clearer as this study continues; here it can be identified as a drive for a more complete life.

In the process of groping, Life has tried many forms; most have proved ineffective and exist no more. Traces of failure are found throughout the geological record. But the record also shows an axis of success. Throughout the ages Life has constructed organisms of ever greater complexity, and with this increased complexity the organism has also shown an increase in consciousness, that is, an increase of intention, of acting with a goal.

In the course of Life's advance, man appeared, or as Teilhard would say, "Thought is born"; life has crossed the threshold of reflection. Man has "emerged from a general groping of the world" (P,189). From Teilhard's first wartime essay onwards man is considered unique in that he reflects. Thus man is integrally part of evolution in that he has risen from the process, but in reflecting on the process he stands apart from it. Thus man is both continuous and discontinuous with evolution. Reflection is defined as "the power acquired by a consciousness to turn in upon itself, to take possession of itself *as an object* . . . no longer merely to know, but to know that one knows" (P,165). In man an organizing unity is formed that is conscious of its own power of organization; this gives rise to abstract logic, reasoned choice, invention and tools. Teilhard quotes a phrase of Julian Huxley: man "is nothing else than evolution become conscious of itself." To this Teilhard would add, "The consciousness of each of us is evolution looking at itself and reflecting upon itself" (P,221). The phrases of Huxley and Teilhard show man as integral to evolution. He is evolution; he is "the point of emergence in nature, at which this deep cosmic evolution culminates and declares itself" (HE,23). But in being able to objectify the process, he also stands apart from it.

The double character by which man is continuous and discontinuous with the process can be illustrated by examples. Man has often been identified as the "tool maker." Teilhard would acknowledge the title, but in it he would see further significance. Throughout the ages the thrust of evolution has been making tools for the animals: claws, horns, wings, and so forth. When man makes a tool he continues that evolutionary thrust of Life. Human invention is "an extension in reflective form" of the basic inventive movement by which life has been advancing from the beginning (P,224). Life has instinctively produced its tools; man also produces his tools, but it is his reflective production of tools that makes man unique. The significance of reflection can also be seen in the transfer of information. What life has learned through experience, it passes on in the gene; what man has learned in experience he passes on reflectively through education. Again man continues reflectively what Life has done from the beginning. But the most significant parallel that Teilhard would draw concerns man's research. The basic movement of life is groping, a tentative reaching out for new and wider syntheses. Man's scientific research is thus the reflective form of groping:

> the instinctive gropings of the first cell link up with the learned groping of our laboratories. So let us bow our heads with respect for the anxieties and joys of "trying all and discovering all." The passing wave that we can feel was not formed in ourselves . . . It reaches us after creating everything on the way. The spirit of research and conquest is the permanent soul of evolution (P,224).

Research is "the highest of human functions" (HE,38); we are moved by "the sacred appetite for research"; people are drawn "irresistibly towards science as to the source of life" (F,20). Just as evolving life seeks to form more extensive physical structures, thought is now groping its way towards forming wider structures of understanding:

> by virtue of human reflection . . . evolution, overflowing the physico-chemical organization of bodies, turns back upon itself and

thereby reinforces itself (. . .) with a new organizing power vastly concentric to the first—the cognitive organization of the universe (P,249).

In rejecting the temptation of matter, Teilhard judged the direction of life to be the direction of increasing truth. The direction was away from the amorphous, and towards ever increasing syntheses. The synthesizing movement of life gives the particles of matter an increased consistency; they are bound into an organism. This synthesizing process is first perceived in the physical world, but it also defines the process of one's inner life. Through scientific research Teilhard was involved in "the cognitive organization of the universe." He was proceeding by a second "organizing power vastly concentric to the first." The noetic groping of man to see, to know, to understand, is the reflective form of the groping of life.

Many people would be inclined to see a total difference between the organization of elements in a biological organism and the organization of elements in the act of comprehension. But it is precisely this difference that Teilhard would deny. If man's conscious power of organization is not in continuity with what has preceeded him, his conscious power of organization would not have evolved. He would only be an observer of evolution and not part of the process itself. Today evolution proceeds by a synthesizing action of the mind. This is why Life and Thought are endlessly linked. Thought is merely the reflective form of Life, Thought is Life squared. "Life (is) carried forward into thought" (V,169). "In man evolution is internalized" (F,221). In writing to a friend Teilhard would ask:

> If "Evolution" shows itself as a process of Arrangement, by what right does one place an absolute division between an arrangement of atoms or neurons and an arrangement of visions, emotions, or sensations? From this point of view, to discover and to know is also to actually extend the Universe ahead and to complete it just as vitalising and socializing it would be (UP,Gignoux,19/June/50).

The very act of knowing is part of the universe; in fact, it is one of the universe's most significant parts. The universe is further extended into Thought in every new way it is known.

Teilhard would draw numerous parallels between Thought and Life:

Thought arises from the individual details of experience. These details could be considered the "atoms" or "grains" of thought. But just as the ultimate particles of matter escape identification, so the ultimate particles of thought are "unapprehensible" (C,99). Facts and details can accumulate in the mind, but beyond this accumulation the mind (evolution's "new organizing power") seeks to draw the details together into a comprehension, a unity wherein each detail is intrinsically bonded to the others. Thought is born! This is "the supreme spiritual act . . . the dust cloud of experience takes on form and is kindled at the fire of knowledge" (AE,9;V,205). Separate facts take on the consistence of an hypothesis; the reversed form of gravity, psychic consistence, has drawn elements together and bonded them by the supreme spiritual act. The new comprehension is more than the sum of the elements; it is the unity itself that is new. As the elements of a living organism are linked at their centers to modify and accentuate one another, so the elements of any truth form a unified whole wherein "the parts support and complement one another ever more effectively" (T,165); "the innumerable elements . . . mutually clarify themselves" (S,39). In the coherence of Thought, we discover again that "unity differentiates."

To form the first living cell, the elements had to reach beyond their individual identity, beyond what was "given." To proceed beyond oneself in hope of sharing in something greater is an act of faith. So Teilhard would ask, "Are not Nature's countless experiments all variants of a single act of faith?" (F,192). The same process is involved when the mind forms a synthesis; it reaches beyond a simple recognition of the "given" of experience. The mind creates and in so doing continues the fundamental work of creation. By faith it creates a unity that is new; "to believe is to form an intellectual synthesis" (C,98). The "supreme spiritual act" is not simply a recognition; each comprehension unites the world in a way that is new. Thus, Teilhard would speak of "the constructive action of Truth" (J,196), or "the Creator role of thought" (UP,Gignoux,19/Jun/50), and appeals to a similar idea suggested by contemporary physics:

> To think "the world" (as physics is beginning to realize) is not merely
> to register it but to confer upon it a form of unity it would otherwise
> (i.e., without being thought) be without (P,249;parenth. in text).

Teilhard would argue that even in mathematics what might ordinarily be termed a discovery is really "the bringing into existence of something new" (P,249). Thus, mathematics is not a presentation of eternal truths; it is an historical process whereby new unities are formed from elements that are old.

Each man has his own experiences, and from these elements he must create "his world." In doing so he confers upon things a unity they would otherwise be without: "each one of us has, in reality, *his own* universe; he is its center and he is called upon to introduce harmony into it" (W,239). Two of Teilhard's essays are entitled "My Universe." That is what each person has, or rather what each person is: a universe wherein the dust of experience is gathered into a unity. This reflective unity is the person; each individual is "the incommunicable expression of a conscious point of view upon the universe" (HE,46 translation amended: "point de vue consciente"). Thus the task for every person is to build his or her soul; that is, each must assemble the widely scattered elements of one's experience into a unified whole. This task is compared to the process of seaweed as it concentrates into its tissues elements found in the expanse of the ocean. Each individual finds in his or her mind traces of all the forces of the universe that have effected him or her, and must work over these forces endlessly. Then, suddenly, from the core of one's spirit a comprehension of the world is born; events are gathered together in "the supreme spiritual act" that again affirms the mysticism of knowledge. The matter comprehended is anything at all—it is only the dust of experience that chance has brought; but it has been seized in an act of creation: "all life, and all thought, is simply the seizing and organizing of chance" (AE,137).

In this work of organization each person is helped by everyone else so that what one might have called "My Universe" becomes increasingly "Our Universe,"—the "Universe of Man," the common world that is developing today particularly through the progress of science. Through this development in understanding, the world itself is becoming more coherent and consistent; it is becoming more true. Some people would object to this way of speaking, they:

> are always contrasting something they call anthropocentric illusion with something they call objective reality. The distinction does not exist. The truth of man is the truth of the universe for man, that is to say, the truth pure and simple (HE,55).

Consequently, when Teilhard writes about the ancient past, he is aware of a certain relativity running through all he says: "I do not pretend to describe them (past ages) as they really were, but rather as we must picture them to ourselves so that the world may be true for us at this moment" (P,35).

Each hypothesis is a tentative effort at rendering coherent "the dust cloud of experience." If a particular hypothesis "succeeds in encircling and harmonizing the world one degree further, we can conclude" that by the hypothesis "we have approached the truth" (HE,54). Hypotheses are the forms of thought, and the many forms of thought are like the many forms of life—they are tentative. And as with the record of life, the record of thought tells of many failures. But as there are axes where life has succeeded, so there are lines along which thought has succeeded: The forms of thought that presently hold up are what we consider the truth. Each age considers its truth to be "*the* Truth," but each truth has its day (MM,114). Various scientific theories have been considered breakthroughs in their time, only to be replaced by later theories. There is a time when a hypothesis unifies experience and is accepted, and a time when it must be renounced lest it prevent a further understanding. Thus, truth as we know it is not final; it is part of a process. It is found in any comprehension that gives coherence to the present data and then leads to a further development, "Coherence and fecundity, the two criteria of truth" (F,189;V,206,227; S,75;J,12/Oct/52). Thus both truth and life are forward-moving processes: "Ideas, like life of which they are the highest manifestation, never turn back" (V,102). Truth, like life, presents itself only "by a series of preliminary trials and gropings" (HE,171). Truth, like life, "can be preserved only by being continually enlarged" (W,140). Like the criterion for life the "criterion of truth, its specific mark, is its power of developing indefinitely" (T,165).

Though one could argue that by his very philosophy Teilhard was presenting a fixed system of truth, Teilhard would refer again to his biological analogy and claim that he does not offer "a definitive framework of truth," rather only "a cluster of axial lines of progression, such as exists and generally comes to light in every evolutionary system" (T,164).

Thus, evolution turns out to be not only the law by which all living organisms have appeared and by which they can be understood; it is also the law by which all ideas have appeared and can be understood. This applies to "chemistry, physics, sociology and even mathematics and the history of religions" (P,219). Though Teilhard's life work as a scientist concerned the evolution of life, when he would try to define evolution he would tell rather of the evolution of thought:

> Is evolution a theory, a system or a hypothesis? It is much more: it is a general condition to which all theories, all hypotheses, all systems must bow and which they must satisfy henceforward if they are to be thinkable and true. Evolution is a light illuminating all facts, a curve that all lines must follow (P,219) . . . Evolution has long ago ceased to be a hypothesis, and become a *general condition of knowledge* . . . (AM,211) . . . evolution . . . has finally *invaded everything* . . . all nuclear physics, all astral physics, all chemistry are in their manner "evolutionary." And the whole history of civilization and ideas is at least as much so (V,246).

The movement of Life has been presented as a guide for the mind, so when an individual would find him- or herself looking to the future with anxiety, Teilhard would urge that he or she consider the relentless advance of life and its record of success in spite of great odds against it (C,106;D,78). This same movement will continue, so it can serve as our guide for the future; "we have only to walk further in the direction in which the lines passed by evolution take on maximum coherence" (P,234). The total coherence of the universe is that to which we are destined, and this total coherence is the Truth in all its fullness, "the total coherence of the universe in relation to each part of itself" (HE,54). This is the direction in which all things grope and the direction in which the mind is groping today. This goal has been present in life through the milennia, now it is present in the human striving to understand. And in the process, whatever is most coherent and most activating is also the most true, "the truth never disarms action," rather it gives an elan, an impetus to the one who knows (S,175;W,231).

Total Truth and Process

When Teilhard acknowledges a final Truth, or speaks of an hypothesis as "closer to the Truth," or sees man engaged in a "quest for Truth" (HU,68), he is allowing for a Truth beyond the process, and towards which the process is moving. To include this total Truth he would speak of the "two halves of truth": there is "the truth come down from heaven" and "the truth developing on earth" (W,75,76, translation of final phrase amended to read in present tense). The Truth from heaven is the total truth that is not yet realized, while the truth developing on earth must continually become ever more comprehensive, for only thereby can our human concepts "attain their true intelligibility" (Li,18).

Because Truth has two halves, people fall prey to a simple error: they judge a stage of the developing truth of earth to be the final Truth come down from heaven. They become "absolute-minded" and set up an absolute system, a cosmos of "geometrical clarity . . . frozen by the light" where there are no "half-lights," where there is "nothing that is not *certain* and *crystal clear*" (W,301;HE,167). Such people will not recognize the amorphousness of matter nor that "around every distinct truth there spreads a penumbra." They have not discovered "the contagion of living truth"; they have allowed "a veil of conventional answers to cover the mystery of life" (HE,19). Thus they remain "the least mystical of men"—for the mystic is drawn to areas where things are "imprecise and boundless." Life itself is imprecise and reaches beyond all bounds, while "the official truth is generally dead" (J,212). People have imposed human bounds on the universe so that it conforms with what they are familiar with and what is ordinary. But by these confines a wide and "fantastic" universe is being concealed. Teilhard would even ask, "Must not truth be extraordinary in order to be true?" (V,229,264).

Teilhard would speak of two types of knowledge (*savoir*): one is an abstract and timeless knowledge of "the world of Ideas and Principles." This he claims to instinctively mistrust. The second is a "real" knowledge that is in constant development; it is "the conscious actuation (that is to say, the prolonged creation) of the universe about us." The first type of knowledge leads to geometry and theology, while the second leads to science and mysticism (Li,269). Thus, mysticism is not based on the possession of a complete truth from heaven; rather it is part of the ongoing process of earth. "Without knowledge and research, there can today be no possibility of . . . real mystical life" (LT,119). The Truth has come down from heaven, but it is a final goal to be reached and as such it is not grasped. But as people grope their way ahead with the advancing truth of scientific research, they sense the heavenly Truth as the ideal to which they proceed.

In his wartime Journal Teilhard considered a basic difficulty that arises when truth is considered an ongoing process.[2] There is a tendency "to make sacred, or taboo, that which is established." But in order that truth advance there first must be a break with the truth that is established. Thus the innovator appears guilty of sacrilege, his or her teaching is suspected or condemned; he or she seems the cause of inquietude and often walks alone. Perhaps such a person hesitates to present what he or she has to say and may even be crushed. Yet unless one breaks with established truth the orthodoxy of tomorrow cannot arise. Put more strongly Teilhard asks, "How can one advance in truth (. . .) without altering that which was provisionally fixed, that is to say, without some sin?" (J,212). There even seems to be "an essential liaison between progress and evil" (J,239); for evil is that which threatens the existing order. The innovator must accept at least the risk of evil and experience some darkness, confusion, and "immediate" evil to come to the truth that will be new. The difficulty seems to reside in the very "mechanism for the acquisition of Truth." Teilhard reflects on the cases of Galileo, Darwin, and even the new biblical criticism. In each case the material evidence presented was seen as a threat to the established orthodoxy and so it was resisted—but it was only in this way that the new orthodoxy could arise.

Only by returning repeatedly to the threatening evidence—the risk of evil—can the veils of convention be removed and the narrowness of vision be opened to the dimensions of God. Teilhard would refer to "physicists" as the mystics, and to research as a sacred duty. The physicists are all those who are wrestling with the amorphousness of matter and with the absurdity of experience that threatens to reduce present comprehensions to dust. These are the mystics, for it is only in the dust that there occurs "the supreme spiritual act," the act "by which the dust cloud of experience takes on form and is kindled at the fire of knowledge" (AE,9;V,205). It takes the threat of disintegration to give rise to the new moment of comprehension, the moment when dust is rendered *Consistent.* Tomorrow what the mystic has to say will constitute an established orthodoxy, but today the mystic knows it as creation and fire.

Teilhard concluded his wartime writings with an imaginative essay that tells of a prophetic figure drawn apart from his fellow man to "follow the way of fire" (HU,59ff). He has become "weary of abstractions, of attenuations, of the wordiness of social life"; now he seeks Reality whole and entire. He heads out to a desert place. There in the distant sky he sees something no larger than a child's hand. It is like "a cloud of gnats dancing in the sun at evening or a whirlwind of dust." It is Matter. Suddenly matter flies at him like an arrow till he is surrounded and invaded by an immense and equivocal power. All about him it vibrates beneath rocks and plants, much as the distant landscape is seen to quiver beyond the overheated soil. Out of the silence Matter speaks and identifies herself:

> I am the love the initiates and the truth
>   that passes away.
> All that compels acceptance and all that
>   brings renewal; all that breaks apart and
>   all that binds together; power, experiment,
>   progress—matter: all this am I (HU,61).

Matter allows that some so-called "wise men" have rejected her with scorn, but they do not get away with this. Their words are at variance with life and they waste away in the narrow outlook to which they confine themselves. They will "die of inanition and their disciples will desert them." Matter faces the prophetic figure as a threatening whirlwind. There is a moment of danger, for matter possesses ambiguous powers that can drag him to the depths or lift him to the skies. Matter challenges man to do battle. Man and matter engage in combat till the prophetic figure feels exhilaration in the conflict. He becomes aware that "all abstract knowledge is a faded reality" compared to the boundless presence he now touches. He sees:

> the ridiculous pretentiousness of human claims . . . to impose on the world the dogmas, the standards, the conventions of man . . . So many things which once had distressed or revolted him—the speeches and pronouncements of the learned, their assertions and their prohibitions, their refusal to allow the universe to move—all seemed to him now merely ridiculous, non-existent . . .

Untamed matter has delivered him from the confines of conventional thought, but only by the severity of its onslaughts. Gradually he comes to bless matter for all it has done for him:

> Blessed are you, harsh matter, barren soil, stubborn rock . . . by constantly shattering our mental categories, (you) force us to go ever further and further in our pursuit of truth. Blessed be you, universal matter . . . by overflowing and dissolving our narrow standards of measurement (you) reveal to us the dimensions of God. . . . Without you, without your onslaughts, without your uprootings of

us, we should remain all our lives inert, stagnant, puerile, ignorant both of ourselves and of God (HU,68–69).

Matter has been identified as the transient (Chapter One); it was because of matter that all things are unstable and threatened with decay. Because of matter each material thing can become other, but in doing so it can escape the limits of its own immanence. Now in the world of human reflection matter is again the threat that breaks down the stability of our concepts. Without matter's senseless intrusions we would have considered ourselves to have found the truth with our first ideas. By its senseless intrusions we find our beliefs are shattered and we are left groping through half-lights, confusion, and the dust of experience. But this groping is precisely what Life has always been doing. Now it is Truth that is groping beyond the confinement of its earlier forms. It may be "the truth that passes away" but as it gropes and feels its way it is slowly expanding to the dimensions of the Truth come down from heaven.

Seeing the Phenomenon of Man within Its Divine Milieu

When Teilhard told of rejecting the *temptation* of matter, life indicated the direction in which to grow in truth and also the direction "to see the light dawn and grow more intense." Having taken this direction the light must have dawned, for Teilhard's wartime writings abound in references to lights, haloes, aureoles and coronas that give these writings a radiant and puzzling quality (see W,253). These lights do not concern interior illuminations, they characterize perceptions of the phenomenal world. Teilhard refused to be absorbed *into* matter, but he did not try to escape *from* it. Matter remained the *milieu* in which he lived. The phenomenon was necessary. It is in terms of phenomenon and milieu (environment) that Teilhard would set his own mysticism in opposition to an earlier form of mysticism that he attributes to unnamed Eastern sages: "Centuries ago the wise men of India were struck by the enslaving and inescapable character of the environment in which human activities were conducted" (F,45). They judged the world to be only "the material trammels that imprison" man, so to maintain and increase their own transcendence they tried to reject the world in its entirety. "Phenomena were regarded as an illusion (Maya) and their connections as a chain (Karma)" (P,211;S,105). To attain a "blessed unity" these sages tried to flee the multiplicity of phenomena. Teilhard wrote an imaginative account of their argument:

> We must persuade ourselves of the non-existence of all surrounding phenomena, destroy the Grand Illusion by asceticism or by mysticism, create night and silence within ourselves; then, at the opposite extreme of appearance, we shall penetrate to what can only be defined as a total negation—the ineffable Reality (F,45).

Teilhard does not object to their desire to escape the world of appearance; he desired to do that himself ("we must break through and go beyond appearances . . . veil . . . without seam" [LT,70,100], etc.) What he objects to in these "Eastern sages" is their attempt to escape *in a "premature fashion."* For Teilhard one must first work with the world of phenomena and escape from it only after "a process of growth" (F,58). We should not try "to escape from things without freeing them at the same time as we free ourselves" (T,46). In the meantime the phenomena need man and man needs the phenomena.

The "Phenomena" can be understood to include only the brute sense data; thus in regards to vision phenomena would comprise only the veneer or "veil" of colors that strike upon the retinas of the two eyes. Teilhard speculates on the moment when we first opened our eyes to the world: "we saw light and things around each of us all jumbled up and on a single plane" (P,216). But since that moment our eyes have developed many additional ways of seeing. Perhaps the first development was when we came to "see" three-dimensionally. Seeing three-dimensionally involves an *interpretation* of the pattern of colors that strikes the retinas. Though one might argue that the mind has added this interpretation to the data in order to render it coherent, the result is that this "interpretation" has subsequently worked its way back into the perception itself so that we "see" differently than before: we *see* three-dimensionally. By developing a whole series of additional "senses" we have gradually built up a more or less coherent way of seeing the world.

The way we see things constitutes our world. Things are seen differently by different individuals. When two people face a landscape what "stands out" for one person is not even noticed by the other. Each individual brings to perception his or her own past experience and future intentions. These affect how and what he or she will see.

This could be illustrated by an example from Teilhard's own life: he *saw* as a paleontologist. A friend who worked with him in the field tells how quickly Teilhard could spot at a distance a stone-tool (a stone shaped by early man) amidst the debris of a gravel bed (Cuénot,156). To all who have not developed a practiced eye the stone would go unnoticed. But to the practiced eye of a paleontologist it lights up with meaning, and all of its precise details begin to shimmer with implications concerning the primitive men who shaped the stone. This is the best way of understanding the haloes and aureoles of which Teilhard spoke. They are the shimmer of meaning, of interrelationships, an object is "seen" to have when it is situated in a context of world events. For centuries these chipped stones had been ignored; it is only through the modern comprehension of evolution that the ancient stone tool can be *seen* as an ancient stone tool. To the untrained eye the scratches and ridges on the stone are insignificant data, but to the practiced eye each detail stands out sharply in terms of its whole context (milieu)—and that milieu is the evolution of man. Reciprocally, the understanding of the evolution of man is modified by this new detail. The detail is grasped only in a context, and the context is then better understood through this detail: "Unity differentiates." The significance of the stone is accentuated, and the story of man's evolution is further nuanced. Through every general understanding countless elements of the world "link together, fall into order and mutually illuminate one another" (S,38–39). But the linking and illumination occur within our human vision. When Teilhard tells of the growing understanding of geological history he writes that its elements "are gaining meaning for our eyes" (V,26). The universe is illumined "to our eyes" (P,48). The frequency of such expressions ("meaning for our eyes," "clear to our eyes," etc.) are the best indication of the significance of both perception and phenomena in the mind of Teilhard.[3]

The point of these recurrent phrases is that Teilhard is dealing with perception and mistrusts any abstract "knowledge" that cannot be *seen* in the phenomena. Such abstract knowledge has become common among educated people today. These educated people readily acknowledge what science says about the age of the earth, about the distances of inter-steller space, and about the structure of the atom. But they have no direct experience of these. Teilhard made his appeal to those who *work* in science, for it is they who come to *see* what science teaches. He would urge his readers who are not involved in science to visit a large museum so that they could at least see rocks, fossils and bones and not simply deal with abstract and mostly inconceivable numbers that are said to tell the age of the earth. But gazing dumbly at rocks and bones is not enough either. We must take what we have come to learn from science and read it back into our sense data so that we perceive differently: we must "educate our eyes." Until we have done this we find "we can look at the night sky year in and year out without ever once making a *real* effort to apprehend the distances and thus the size of the sidereal masses" (P,91).[4] We might acknowledge the reality of evolution, but our eyes do not see it taking place everywhere about us; we might acknowledge that God is present everywhere, but our eyes have not yet learned to *see* Him. We need again "a training of the eyes."

Teilhard understood the bulk of his philosophical and religious writings as ways to train the eyes. He introduced his first essay as an attempt "to make men see" (W,15,see W253), and this continued throughout his writing. *The Divine Milieu* was presented as "a way of teaching how to see" (D,46). *The Phenomenon of Man* was introduced as an effort "to see and make others see," "to try to see". *The Phenomenon of Man* tells of the "effort to see," and urges that we must "make our eyes see." What Teilhard is trying to see and make others see is what happens when man is not considered in abstraction but is placed "within the framework of phenomenon and appearance" (P,31).

In placing man in such a framework Teilhard does not mean the flat veneer of colors that strike the retinas. Rather he wants to show the meaning that haloes man when he is placed in the context of a vast cosmic movement. Generally, one sees a human event only in the perspective of the present, the immediate environment, and human society. But Teilhard would argue that one such dislocated event cannot be understood at all; he would argue that if human society itself is not seen as a part of nature but isolated from the living world that gave it birth, it begins to appear artificial and incoherent. Both man and human society can and must be understood in terms of the universe:

> Each and every one of us, if we care to observe it, is enveloped—is haloed—by an extension of his being as vast as the universe. We are conscious of only the core of ourselves (W,253).

To present what he would call "the whole phenomenon of man" Teilhard devoted the first half (about 150 pages) of *The Phenomenon of Man* to the evolution of the earth *before* man's appearance; for it is only in the total context of an evolving cosmos that the present human phenomenon is intelligible. Thus the chemistry of oceans hundreds of millions of years ago partially determined the blood content of the fish who swam there. These fish have passed this inheritance on to us, their descendants. To understand human blood, one must see it in the whole context from which it arose. The movements of our primate ancestors through the trees has effected the bone structure of the human hand; the whole refinement of the instincts and the long development of ideas has given rise to our present thoughts. The result is that:

> In each one of us, through matter, the whole history of the world is in part reflected. And however autonomous our soul, it is indebted to an inheritance worked upon from all sides—before ever it came into being—by the totality of the energies of the earth (D,59).

Thus we can understand ourselves and the whole phenomenon of man only in the context of the entire evolving earth.

Each person is more or less sensitive to a level of social sensibilities. Through this sensitivity one comes to see a structure of meaning "haloing" the different individuals who make up his world; they are part of the milieu in which he lives. Apart from this familiar milieu, strangers are seen as "strangers"—perhaps even seen as threatening aliens whom we resent or fear. This is a limitation of our vision that has given rise to various feelings of nationalism. But even if our halo of meaning is extended to include all humanity, it would still be incomplete; for in seeing only the human milieu we are not seeing our vast cosmic halo, the extension of our being which is "as vast as the universe." My own body is not a certain quantity of cells that I possess totally—for I have no such possession of the body I call my own. The whole cosmos was involved in making it what it is and will continue to affect it regardless of what I might do. But in return I will affect the entire cosmos by whatever I do. Thus: "*My* matter is not a *part* of the universe that I possess *totaliter:* it is the *totality* of the Universe possessed by me *partialiter*" (S,13).

Teilhard often alludes to Pascal's feelings of anxiety before the dimensions of space (the very large and the very small) revealed by newly invented telescopes and microscopes (Pascal: "These two abysses frighten me."). When faced with the macrocosm and the microcosm the whole human enterprise can fade into oblivion and insignificance. This again causes the distress of multiplicity: the entire human mileiu is *seen* only as an isolated unit clashing with worlds wholly alien. It is the distress that gives rise to nationalism: one's own human group is seen only as an isolated nation clashing with nations wholly alien. Pascal's abysses of the immense and the infinitesimal are distressful only to those who *see* them as alien; that is, only to those who do not see them as *part of their own being.* In Teilhard's effort "to see and to make others see" the whole phenomenon of man, he is trying to show man as the center of a cosmic tide that has been gathering into the human throughout the vast abysses of space and time. That is, he is trying to extend our perception of "the halo" of meaning until the human milieu is seen as the universal milieu, for "Each of us is enveloped—is haloed—by an extension of his being as vast as the universe." By seeing man extending beyond the "merely human," the structures of society lose some of their artificial quality and the activities of man are seen to be part of the basic current of the cosmos. Thus man's scientific gropings are *seen* to link up with the gropings of Life throughout the long ages. Thus man is not seen as alien to the universe; he is *seen* as integral to it, he is even seen as central to it.

The previous section of this chapter outlined an imaginative essay of Teilhard concerning a prophetic traveler wandering in a desert and encountering matter untamed. There he came to realize "the ridiculous pretensions of human claims to impose on the world . . . conventions of man." He took pity on those "who take fright at the span of a century or those whose love is bounded by the frontiers of a nation." By his experience of the physical world he finds "a *point d'appui,* he had found refuge, *outside* the confines of human society." It is through this contact with the powers of matter that he is freed from "all that is *artificially contrived,* all that is merely *human* in humanity" (HU,66).

Anyone's vision is artificially contrived if he sees man as "merely human" and the physical world as "merely physical." There has even developed a whole "science of man as marginal to the universe" and a whole "science of the universe without man" (V,162). Both are artificial contrivances that leave both man and the universe isolated and unintelligible. Teilhard would even claim that the cause of all our intellectual and moral difficulties is that "the scientist himself stands apart from the objects of science" (HE,20). This standing-apart renders the objective universe natural and inert and the consciousness of man isolated and artificial; so "our view of life is obscured and inhibited by the absolute division that we continually place between the natural and the artificial"

(V,59). When the traveler went to the untamed desert he was not rejecting humanity and the whole juridical-moral milieu formed by humanity. He was only rejecting the artificial quality that juridical, moral and personal qualities are *seen* to have when they are not seen as part of the total natural movement of the cosmos. The universe is the milieu from which man has arisen and wherein he must be understood: "to understand man is to have understood the universe and vice versa." Again, "unity differentiates"; a unified view of the universe will clarify the nature of man. The universe is needed to illumine man and man is needed to illumine the universe.

Man's evolving consciousness must be seen as integral to the physical world and the physical world must be seen as integral to man's desire to know. Since man is seen as matter become reflectively conscious, this understanding should change our whole perception of matter. Matter has generally been assumed to be wholly inert, devoid of all consciousness. But in acknowledging that our own reflective awareness has evolved out of the physical world, we should begin to reappraise our understanding of matter. Again, we might acknowledge man's evolutionary origin, but it is all abstract—we retain a limitation on our vision. Man still *appears* to be an alien visitor on the planet that bore him and often senses himself to be an alien spirit within the matter he calls his own body. Teilhard would argue that in order to have a coherent understanding of man-cosmos one must begin by assuming a minute trace of consciousness present in all matter. Most people regard consciousness as a property present only in animals and man; there it is seen to be "an exception," a quality that applies only to a small sector of matter. But Teilhard asks where would modern physics be if at the beginning of the present century it had dismissed the discovery of the Curies concerning the atomic decay of radium as "an exception." The discovery of the Curies caused much confusion in physics, but eventually it was integrated into the physicists' understanding of matter and it revolutionized that understanding. Teilhard would argue that matter-reflectively-conscious is a fact that each of us knows, and this fact should also be integrated into a broadened understanding of physics. Again, it is a fact that would revolutionize our understanding:

> Man appears to be an exception. Why not, then, make him the key of the universe? Man refuses to allow himself to be forced into a

mechanistic cosmogony. Why not, then, construct a physics whose starting point is spirit? (C, 105–106).

Teilhard believed that eventually science would be forced "to build its explanations of the experiential world on the spirit" (LT, 159). Thus when the first 150 pages of *The Phenomenon of Man* talk about matter before the coming of man, it is a different understanding of matter than is ordinarily assumed; it is matter seen in terms of what it is coming to be. For "by learning to focus his vision more correctly," man is beginning to see that the depths of past ages were "in reality filled by himself" (S, 132). Through this focus of his vision:

> man ceases to be a spark fallen by chance on earth and coming from another place. He is the flame of a general fermentation of the universe which breaks out suddenly on the earth. He is no longer a sterile enigma or discordant note in nature. He is the key of things and the final harmony. In him everything takes shape and is explained (HE, 23–24).

Because Teilhard sees an intrinsic unity between man and nature he would often use expressions that link the two orders: man is referred to as "hominized earth" or "hominized nature" (S, 94). Teilhard would write of a universe "whose stuff is personality" (HE, 73). He would bring concepts from thermodynamics into psychology (AE, 361). He would speak of a "physics of the spirit," and the "physical realness of thought" (LT, 150); of faith as a "physical power," (W, 237) and love as a factor of "physical construction" (W, 171). Since the human experience of love is drawing the cosmos together, Teilhard would urge that we deal with the energies of love as if we were engineers. If such phrases sound disconcerting and unpoetic, it is good to recall that the most quoted and perhaps the most poetic passage of Teilhard suggests a continuity between the physical and the personal:

> The day will come when, after harnessing the ether, the winds, the tides, gravitation, we shall harness for God the energies of love. And, on that day, for the second time in the history of the world, man will have discovered fire (T, 87).

In all of these expressions Teilhard is trying to eliminate the absolute separation generally assumed between the physical and the psychic, between matter and consciousness. It is evident that taking terms from one context and applying them indiscriminately to another could lead to many absurdities. But it is also good to recall that we are living in a *uni*verse; that love is both psychic and physical—as is everything else in our lives: in order to think or pray we must eat, and what we eat affects both our thought and prayer. Thus many of the distinctions between physics, chemistry, biology, psychology and philosophy are only distinctions because of the different methodologies that are used. Teilhard would even see value in these distinctions and warn that the different disciplines should not merge; they should continue "to assail the real from different angles" (P,30;D,117). But some attempt should be made to form a unified science. Teilhard was excited by his visit to the cyclotron at Berkeley and delighted to find those working there unsure if they were "engaged in research, or in industry, in physics or metaphysics, in energetics or medicine" (AE,352).

For Teilhard the artificial separation between man and the cosmos is at the root of the contemporary moral confusion (HE,20). If man is considered only in his present context, his basic moral task of building a new humanity cannot even be understood. It is only through a deep feeling for man's past and the past of the cosmos that one can begin to envision the new humanity that can be formed in the future. In the final years of Teilhard's life he often spoke of organizing a symposium on man, but he was insistent on not wanting any "humanists" or "anthropologists" to attend. Because the humanists "make of Man a world apart" and thus for Teilhard there is "no greater enemy of the science of man." The anthropologists present "Man studied as a world apart (or as a sub-world) *not* as the prolongation of the cosmic process" (UP,Huxley,1/Apr/ 52;J,22/Apr/54). Humanists and anthropologists might acknowledge man's evolution, but they have not had a "training of the eyes" that allows them to conceive of man as a prolongation of the cosmic process.

But even when one comes to see the humano-cosmic phenomenon, the whole phenomenon of man is not yet understood, for our vision of man-cosmos is still incomplete. Just as our vision of the world is shaped by past experience, so it is shaped by our future expectations. Through educating our eyes we have come to see all things rising to increased consciousness throughout the ages. But if we also believe that life will ultimately stop short of fulfillment because it will be overtaken by entropy, then the world is *seen* to be futile in all it does; all strivings are seen to be absurd as they lead nowhere. Vision is affected and we find "the paralyzing poison of death eats irresistibly into everything" (AE,400). But if, on the contrary, we believe that all things find fulfillment in God, then the universe is seen to make sense. Thus fulfillment in God constitutes "the only true point of view from which the world can be understood" (D,125). If we believe in ultimate fulfillment (as opposed to ultimate frustration) and believe in final intelligibility (as opposed to final absurdity), we begin to *see* a different world, a world in which "the poison of universal death has vanished from the heart of all things" (AE,401). "It is the humano-cosmic phenomenon which, by reaction, is profoundly modified in our eyes" (AE,146). The "humano-cosmic phenomenon" is what constitutes the universal milieu; this phenomenon is "profoundly modified in our eyes," that is, the universal milieu is seen to be the divine milieu (humano-cosmic-divine). Just as we came to see three-dimensionally, or see as paleontologists when our understanding affected our vision, so now we begin to *see* as believers. This final training of the eyes must come from God. It is his gift. We say we believe, yet it is often only an abstraction and we walk in darkness. We turn to God in prayer: "Lord, we know and feel that you are everywhere around us; but it seems that there is a veil before our eyes" (D,132).

Perhaps the moment of living faith comes upon us suddenly—like a breeze passing in the night. "God reveals himself everywhere"; He is "perceived by our eyes"; "the world is lit with God"; we have a "perception of the divine spread everywhere"; a "perception of the divine omnipresence" (D,131). Everything appears "more fragrant, more colored, more intense." All things possess a deep brilliance, yet their individuality is "accented in meaning" (D,130). The divine illumination has retained and exalted "all that is most specific" (D,118). All things are united in God, but at the same time God "pushes to its furthest possible limit the differentiation among the creatures he concentrates in himself" (D,116). Thus for the final time—"unity differentiates." First, this characterized the unity formed by life, then the unity formed by thought; now it is true of the unity of all things in God. All things have gained final consistency. They are united, and by our act of faith the unity is *perceived:*

> the higher reality of the supernatural world is apparent only to those
> who have the courage to make up their mind it is true. . . . The

vision of faith accompanies (or should I say 'follows'?) *the action of faith.* Like other real objects, Christ is "experienced" (W,245–246).

The act of faith renders the veil transparent and Christ is seen to be everywhere:

> the man who *dares* to believe reaches a sphere of created reality in which things, while retaining their habitual texture, seem to be made out of a different substance . . . at the same time everything becomes luminous, animated, instinct with love. Through the operation of faith Christ appears (W,246).

The entire world of the phenomenon is Christified by our faith; Christ "in whom all things hold together" is seen as the completion of the phenomenon of man. Christ is seen as "the physical center of creation" and "everything around us is physically Christified" (S,59). Everything is changed for the believer:

> If we believe, then everything is illuminated and takes shape around us: chance is seen to be order, success assumes an incorruptible plenitude, suffering becomes a visit and a caress of God. . . . The immense hazard and the immense blindness of the world are only an illusion to him who believes. *Fides substantia rerum* (D,136–137;MM,232).

Fides Substantia Rerum

Teilhard alludes to many passages in the Gospels wherein Jesus speaks of faith accomplishing something: it heals, makes whole, moves mountains, and it overcomes the world. Thus, faith can be identified as an efficient or operative power. Teilhard considers various ways that this operative power might be understood. First, he allows that there is some truth in the saying, *Fortuna favet fortibus:* those who believe they will succeed have an extra self-confidence and thus an additional power to do so. Then, Teilhard considers Christian Scientists and various psychics who claim that the believing mind can exert a mental influence on present and future events. Teilhard allows that they do have a real power, but he judged their power to be only a natural power that could do nothing beyond ameliorating the present life.[5] What Teilhard was seeking was a faith that would truly overcome the world, a faith that brought a final salvation completely out of reach of any natural power (W,233,234,237;D,129).

Still this faith must be rooted in the natural process as a power that both "molds . . . the physical system of the universe" and involves no "violation of nature's laws."

Before one can understand how Teilhard would consider faith an operative power, one must first acknowledge the Idealist nature of his thought. Throughout the history of philosophy most philosophers have been unwilling to consider themselves Idealists—it is usually their commentators who have given them the title. Teilhard also had some reticence with the title, but he often expressed sympathy for Idealism and a corresponding sympathy helps in understanding his writings. When Teilhard wrote his first essay and told of his "reversal," he claimed that Idealist thinkers had proposed philosophies similar to what he had found hinted at in experience: "Everything that exists has a basis of Thought" (W,41). He would later allow that his own thinking "accorded particularly well with an 'Idealist' metaphysic," but he would add that his thinking did not depend on such (Li,92). At one point he would term his own philosophy "scientific idealism," and then define the phrase to mean "matter being malleable by the mind that informs it" (HE,114;see W,235).

Teilhard referred to Idealist thinkers immediately after the account of his "reversal," for by his reversal he shifted from a pantheism of Matter to a pantheism of Form. In identifying Being with Form the world was based on Thought; evolution became primarily the evolution of ideas, and the psychic phenomena became *the* phenomena, the "true phenomena." The world of Matter was left close to the edge of nothingness (see the previous chapter) or secondary at best (it was "an ephemeral by-effect" of consciousness!)—(AE,393;J,196). Years later he would further justify the reversal by pointing to speculations of modern physics wherein matter is shown to be not at all the "stable essence of the world" it had long been considered, rather, it is only an "ever closer approximation of nothingness" (S,29,50). In a vague reference to modern physics he would claim, "The atoms themselves broke up under the impact of radio-active energies" (HE,174). The result is that the materialists are said to have lost their "fixed lower point." This is seen as a reason for physicists turning from materialism to a recognition of the primacy of Thought. What these theories of physics are said to reveal is not an ultimate unbreakable particle of matter; rather, what they reveal—in phrases that would make one think of Plato or Kant—is "the intellectual texture of the investigator's mind beneath the shifting patterns of his phenomena" (HE, 114). Thus, "in what remained of phenomena" the mind cannot detect "anything but the forms that it had itself imposed on them" (HE, 174). This is Teilhard's Idealism and it is what he means by claiming that the world is based on Thought : "I am always somewhat disconcerted when I meet someone who does not see that the World cannot exist other than based on Thought" (Li, 88). Matter itself is seen to be "insubstantial." At the same time Thought is the intelligible form that the mind has been using to interpret the phenomena and this is what it ultimately discovers. Discovery of the world is ultimately self-discovery! "In the final issue, mind found itself once again face to face with its own reflection" (HE, 174). Since matter is a mirror, discovery of the world is ultimately self-discovery or discovery of God. Thus Teilhard would bless matter —not for what it tells about itself—but because without it we would remain "ignorant both of ourselves and of God" (HU, 69).

Teilhard has often claimed that the universe is made of "spiritual stuff" and that science must "build its explanation of the experiential world on the spirit" (LT, 159), and so forth. But readers of the English text must recall that Teilhard used the French world *esprit;* this is generally translated as "spirit," but it can also be rendered as "mind." This has sometimes been done; but perhaps it would be more accurate if it were done more generally. Teilhard would seem to resolve the ambiguity of the French word in his introduction of neologisms from the Greek: "Noosphere," and "Noogenesis" rather than "Pneumasphere" and "Pneumagenesis." Translating *esprit* as mind gives his writings a different cast: the universe is made of "mental stuff"; we must take a "new step in the genesis of mind"; and "the supreme happiness that I had formerly looked for in iron was to be found only in Mind." It will then be on *Mind* that Christ will bestow his everlasting Form!! Teilhard's mysticism is truly one of knowledge.

Just as Teilhard argued for a "reversal" since matter is involved in endless disintegration "downwards"—that is, away from mind—so Teilhard would see a similar endless disintegration as one looks back into the past. In either case one is going against the movement of evolution and thereby moving towards a pure multitude that is lost to all human comprehension (P, 39; S, 46). However, in the movement of evolution the multitude of particles is metamorphising itself "into Psyche"; it is transforming itself "into Thought" (HM, 28). Or even in a more Idealistic

phrase: "The universe transforms itself into an Idea (Noogenesis)"
(J,25/Mar/52). Thus the whole of evolution can be understood as "nothing
but an immense psychic exercise" (HE,23). All things are striving to
become Thought, that is, they are striving to be known by man, for the
universe's "final state of equilibrium is in *being thought*" (T,165;W,138).
As Thought, each being will attain its "higher form of existence"; "fuller
being is to be found . . . in the increasing domination of the world by
Thought" (S,81). Man's task is "to give things their highest possible
degree of reality . . . in his knowledge of them" (W,139). The human
world is identified in terms of this function; it is the "zone of continuous
spiritual transformation wherein all inferior realities" are sublimated into
psychic realities and this process is ultimately "a sort of vast ontogenesis"
(D,61,124). Man is that wherein the world comes into fuller being in
being known:

> since the world can only fulfill itself insofar as it expresses itself in a
> systematic and reflective perception. . . . some physical consumma-
> tion of things is bound up with the explicit perception we make of
> them (P,249).

The Idealism of Teilhard could be identified as an Idealism of the
future: "the universe transforms itself into an Idea." The process is still
taking place and only at the end will there be a unified world of ideas.
Matter itself is insubstantial and it will disappear except for the universal
comprehensions humanity has formed by working with matter. All that
will remain is a thinking without a brain (AM,264). Thus Teilhard would
seem to propose an eventual Platonism; the World of Forms is in the
making. Teilhard would even write of a Neo-Platonism of Evolution and
consider writing an essay titled, "Platonism Evolutionized."[6] Because
Teilhard speaks in eloquent praise of Matter, he is generally not
considered a Platonist. But when he speaks of the material world
reflecting form from on high, he does not seem far from Plato's
understanding of participation. Teilhard would even speak of matter as
"interposed between our minds and the world of essences" (HU,69).
Matter does not separate us from the "world of essences"; it is only by
working our way through matter that our minds can expand to the
dimensions of the universe and true universals. The journey through
matter cannot be cut short for us any more than it could be for Plato (*The*

Philebus). Apart from this one reference Teilhard does not seem to have spoken elsewhere of "the world of essences," but these essences often seem to be implied in the curious abstract quality his thought can have. It often sounds as if he is writing about Platonic Forms when he writes of Humanity, Atomicity, The Centric, and so forth. This impression is furthered by the abundant use of capitalization in the French texts; they are often reduced in the English. Even Woman is "universalized" as Teilhard tells of The Feminine ("The Universal Feminine," "The Eternal Feminine," etc.). The extent of his "Platonism Evolutionized" can be seen in an essay on love that ends by claiming that "Sexuality for the man will be satisfied by pure womanliness" (HM,61;W,192;HE,77). Platonism is also suggested when Teilhard speaks of Christ: Christ was presented as the final Form of the World and as the one who has already impressed upon it certain *formae cosmicae*. Then, instead of saying that the world will be united with a supreme Person, Teilhard writes that it will be united with "the Supreme *Personal*." He generally spoke of "the Universal Christ" and titled his final essay even more abstractly, "The Christic." In "The Christic" he further compounded abstractions by writing of "Christic Cosmicity"!!! (HM,94;see HM,39,80;Li,309).

Teilhard was aware of this generalizing tendency in his writing: he tells of being fascinated by "the Impersonal and the Generalized," and would explain, "My irresistible tendency is to universalize what I love, because otherwise I cannot love it" (HM,58,201). But Teilhard would also indicate that "to universalize" has a very different meaning for him than it has for Plato or the Mediaeval Scholastics (AM,224,269;J,3/Sep/52;UP, Gignoux,19/June/50).

The Scholastics spoke frequently of essences or universals and understood them to be abstract sets of qualities that God might or might not choose to create: "man," "angel," "flying horse," etc. The Platonist spoke of ideals "recollected" from another world. For Teilhard the universal qualities developed by modern science are seen as radically different as they do not concern abstract *possibilities*. They involve a *perception* of the physical world, and (as was explained in the previous section) they are *seen* in the phenomena. Thus they form "a new type of Universal that was not visible to the Scholastics." When Teilhard refers to "Humanity" or "Man," he is not considering an abstract essence, but a "mega-organism developing a collective soul." The reality of Humanity is what the modern world is only beginning to perceive. It is not an abstraction but a political fact and a social force in today's world. Humanity was not so perceived and as such it did not exist in ancient Greece or Mediaeval Europe. It has required a vast technological development for it to be perceived and realized; thus, it can be called a "new type of Universal that was not visible to the Scholastics." It is not something that a Platonist could "recollect" from another world as it does not exist in another world. Rather, it is constitutive of this world. Humanity is a perception which at the same time actualizes what it perceives: Humanity exists and exists only in the perception of its unity—much as a nation only exists in the people's perception of themselves as a nation. Thus, the perception furthers the reality of the perceived for it unifies it in a new way; this unifying perception is itself a prolongation of the act of creation (Li, 269). The universe itself acquires the unity that each man gives it by his perception of it, and it is unified differently by each individual.

Teilhard refers to an imaginative short story by R.H. Benson that tells of a man coming to a lonely chapel where a nun is at prayer. The man begins to see the whole world moving and organizing itself around the intensity of the tiny praying figure; it seems that the nun "animated all things" (D, 133). Cosmic immensities gathered about her while she acted as unifying center and intimate substance of them all. For Teilhard, each man and woman is such a unifying center; thus, "the material world can today be seen by us as suspended from the spiritual consciousness of men" (S, 47). Since each person *is* a particular way that the world has become centered, what each person does is really what the world does at one of its centers. When a person makes an act of faith in the transcendent God, his own center passes out of himself or herself into God; then, all the things he or she has united become centered on God. Each man and woman is like the nun, who had animated all things; now all things are animated by God through the individual. The basic insubstantiality of things had acquired a limited substantiality in being known by the individual ("Everything that exists has a basis of Thought"). Now things become fully substantial when the Thought that has unified them is centered on God. Thus, faith is termed the substance of things (*fides substantia rerum*, a phrase taken from the Epistle to the Hebrews 2:1). In terms of the diagram presented in Chapter One, human knowledge is the passage of elements F, G, H and I to point A; faith is the passage of point A to point Ω. By an act of faith an individual center of the world has entered into

God; faith is the operative power by which this occurs. It is faith that gives indestructibility to the fragility of the world.

My present identity is constituted by all that I have experienced. When I make an act of faith, all that I have experienced enters God. "In the act in which I give myself to God I pass altogether—with all the details of my past" (Li,42). Through the act of faith I find that all the events of my past life are perceived differently; they all take on a sharpness of meaning; the world in which I *have* lived is now seen as possessing a luminous quality, for the central essence of this world has been eternalized in God. A world has been saved from meaninglessness and decay: "In each soul God loves and partly saves the whole world which that soul sums up in an incommunicable and particular way" (D,60). Yet the power by which faith has operated is in conformity with the laws of nature; faith is the continuation and completion of the striving of all things. Things had gained a first soul with the appearance of man; now "all the natural links of the world remain intact," but an "additional soul" is given them; they have become "super-animated" by God. It is through faith that all things have become "more fully animate," "animated by a new finality"; by our faith Christ has become "the higher soul within things" (D,136;W,257–58). But Christ animates all things only insofar as men believe; it is by faith that Christ is operative. It is by faith that the world is "haloed" and made whole. Without faith the world is stripped of its substance and disintegrates.

This study has tried to show that when Teilhard considered knowledge, he always meant perception. Perhaps he could be best identified as a phenomenologist. When he speaks of faith and urges that without it the world is without substance and disintegrates, he is saying what any person experiences when he or she is unable to believe. As long as one "lives by faith" the world is *seen* to be alive and animated by the presence of God. When faith is weak the world is *seen* to be governed by blind chance, the sky appears dark and the waters shifting. Faith is the *operative power* that makes all the difference:

> The first time a man says "I believe," nothing outside his own soul appears to alter. In fact, through the words he has spoken, that man has produced a reaction in universal Reality . . . all created powers are transformed, as though by magic, *in the circle of which he is the*

center. Natural forces, hitherto alien, hostile or ambivalent, are without exception straightaway charged *for him* with the influence of Christ . . . the whole impact of the world . . . takes on Christ in its inner substance . . . the whole impact of things . . . brings a contact with Christ; he feels in them the touch of Christ's hand . . . *Credenti omnia convertuntur in Christum* (W,257–58).

The final phrase of this quotation is a modified rendition of a phrase in Paul's Epistle to the Romans (8:28): "For those who love God all things work together unto good" (see W,238;MM,92). Teilhard modified this to affirm that for those who believe all things work together unto Christ. By faith Christ becomes present, visible and tangible. In faith he is *seen* as the soul of everyone we meet and the soul of every event. Everything we touch is animated by him—but only if we believe.

Perhaps this way of perceiving the Universal Christ is easy so long as we are alive to the fullness of life and things are going our way. But this is not the story of anyone's life—and *it is good that it is not.* An earlier section of this chapter told of a liaison between progress and evil. There, scientific truth was seen to progress only by unforeseen and stubborn facts that would dislodge scientists from the "truth" they seemed to know, while at the same time leaving them in confusion and darkness. In a similar way, an individual can make progress and grow only if unforeseen events thwart his or her intentions and introduce a confusion that forces the person to seek a wider context for his or her life. We all work with a vague sense that someday a disastrous event may happen to us: fire, pestilence, storms, earthquakes or dark moral forces can sweep away in one moment all that we have been trying to do with our lives. In such "moments of absurdity" we question the whole process of trying to understand life at all and we see no possibility for a "mysticism of knowledge." We are tempted to surrender to a radical ignorance of self, of God, and of the world. Yet the comprehensive power of faith is strong; it stubbornly seeks to form a wider *consistence* out of the shambles of a previous faith; "and the more threatening and irreducible reality appears, the more firmly and desperately must we believe" (D,137). If we continue to believe and only *if* we continue to believe, the horrible thing itself undergoes a change; no matter how frightening it has appeared, it is suddenly seen as—Christ; "the most obscure and most hateful part of the world becomes the most luminous and divine of all" (S,73). The Christ "we see is Christ crucified" (W,208). To *see* that it is Christ involves more than a human way of seeing. We are asked to transcend the human; the process will not be wholly strange as Life has always been transcending itself. This transcending is seen as a natural process. Faith is the operative power that extends the natural process.

Events in the life of Teilhard were often difficult and disappointing; he was misunderstood, silenced, and sent into exile. But he tells of trying to see each of these events as the touch of Christ. When religious superiors sent him to China he wrote, "If I cease to *believe* foolishly in the animation of all things *for me* by Our Lord . . . the world will fall into powder" (Li,132). It is faith alone that can render the dust of events a substance. When Teilhard first heard of the atomic bomb he kept repeating again and again: *"Il faut croire, il faut croire."* On many occasions he wrote letters of consolation to others in their time of grief. The consolation he offered was always the same: the tragic death or illness they have experienced is really the adorable Christ—if they believe it is so. In fact, "everything that happens is adorable" (LT,183,288,294;UP, Arsenne Henry,24/Nov/43;Li,350–51).

"Credenti omnia convertuntur in Christum." It is faith that changes everything. This is what faith has always done: it was through faith that cells first proceeded out of themselves to form a multicelled organism; it is through faith that thought proceeds out of its old form to confront the dust of experience and hopefully create a new truth ("to *believe* is to effect a new synthesis"); it is through faith that the shattering events of any individual's life can be confronted and finally unified *as* Christ; it is by faith that "little by little, we shall see the universal horror unbend, and then smile upon us, and then take us in its more-than-human arms." The immense hazard and blindness of the universe disappear, for they "are only an illusion to him who believes. *Fides, substantia rerum"* (D,137).

Chapter Three

AN EXPLOSION OF DAZZLING FLASHES
The Conjunction of All and Person

Teilhard tells of always being dominated by a passion for the Absolute. But as a young boy he was aware of this Absolute in two conflicting ways: "At one time it would be a piece of metal; at another, I would take a leap to the other extreme and find satisfaction in the thought of God-Spirit" (HM,197). As seen in Chapter One the piece of metal rusted and his interest turned to rocks and the universe. He would term this interest the first focus (*foyer*) of his soul. At the other extreme was the focus of "God Our Lord, revealed end of the Universe." Confused by the two foci his soul felt caught "*between two absolutes:* that of experience (the Universe) and that of Revelation (transcendent God)" (HM,207; italics and parentheses in text). As a young Jesuit he considered setting aside his interest in rocks so that he might be a more dedicated priest. His spiritual director advised him to continue with both interests, which he did without much understanding how this would be possible. Later, he became famous as a priest-geologist living in two different worlds with very different assumptions. But in the meantime the two foci had come together in the depths of his soul "in an explosion of dazzling flashes" (HM,50; AE,381).

Two Stars

The two foci occur frequently in the writings of Teilhard; they are often called two stars, (W,184,300;S,121;C,66,75,147;D,47,52;T,95–97,157; HE,159;AE,381;HM,214, 218–19), two rival stars, two divine stars, two worlds, two suns, etc. They exert contrary attractions: the religion of earth and the religion of heaven (S, 120); the sense of earth and the sense of God (F, 83); the passion for the world and the passion for God (Li, 137); communion with earth and communion with God (W, 28–57); the pagan beauty of the earth and the Christ of the Gospels (D, 46–47). But beyond the contrary attractions Teilhard would offer to show "how easily the two stars whose divergent attractions" disorganize one's faith can be "brought into conjunction" (D, 47).

In his first essay ("Cosmic Life"), Teilhard presented the attractions as two communions: Communion with Earth and Communion with God. Each communion has both a value and a limitation: Communion with Earth puts one into the tangible world wherein he is invigorated and challenged. He is encouraged by the strivings of his fellow man and feels called upon to dedicate himself to the great work of humanity. He is stimulated by his work though it does involve great personal sacrifice —but he soon finds a lament rising from the depths of his soul: in the work to which he is dedicated his own human person does not seem to count. He is losing himself for an impersonal society of the future; the whole charm of life is being lost in the production of a distant and "faceless Divinity." In his work he is losing the "mysterious flower" that is his incommunicable self. To achieve communion with the evolving earth, he has had to submerge or sacrifice himself.

Then he turns in the opposite direction: communion with the revealed God. The great charm of Christianity is that it is "above all a religion of persons, the religion of souls." In a deeply personal moment the soul accepts the tender words of God and is no longer lost in a vast impersonal universe, rather it is incorporated forever into the company of saints, the Kingdom of Heaven. This brings delight to the soul, but now the mind experiences a "stumbling block": the grandeurs and promises immanent to the world of experience seem to count for nothing. There seems to be a rift "between heaven's design and the earth's most noble ambitions." Each of the communions is found to be incomplete, and each possesses what the other lacks. The dilemma is resolved by a "Communion with God through the Earth," and from this first essay onwards the spirituality of Teilhard is *through the earth*. This is the way the two stars will be reconciled.

The same two appeals are found in *The Phenomenon of Man*: Teilhard speaks at length and with enthusiasm concerning what science can do to bring mankind to a unity and utopia on earth. But then he points to the reality of the present century wherein similar ideals have been proposed but have led to dissension and totalitarian states. Marxists speak of the coming of a workers' utopia. They speak as though all the sufferings throughout the ages were justified so that the future Humanity can gather an acquisition of industries, discoveries, ideas and works of art (P,261). But Teilhard objects that if that is all that will be gathered from our labor there will be a colossal wastage. The works we will leave behind will be only a shadow of our real selves. Our soul "is obviously not something of which we can dispossess ourselves for the benefit of others as we might give away a coat or pass on a torch. For we are the very flame of that torch" (P,261). Such again is the soul's lament. Marxism is urging humanity to cooperate in the great work immanent in the total earth. Its totalitarian ideal has the appeal of the universal, but it has resulted in man being in fetters. The person is ignored. The mechanized society that Communism has produced is " 'the Million' scientifically assembled. The Million in rank and file on the parade ground; the Million standardised in the factory,"—the result would lead one to believe that "it is mechanization that seems to emerge inevitably from totalization" (P,257). This depersonalization seems part of the All, the all of total society in which one is supposed to merge. Many continue to believe in the All, but they do so at great expense. Teilhard observed that "our world denies personality and God because it believes in the All: Everything depends on convincing it that, on the contrary, it *must* believe in the personal because it believes in the All" (HE,72).

Just as Teilhard would criticize impersonal societies, so he would criticize a formalized Christianity that is so concerned with the transcendent and personal that it presents itself in extrinsic and juridical terms. The statements of dogma often seem to be apart from all experience, "above" the universe with no connection to it (W,250). In highly personal categories God is described as a Father who "rules, fosters, pardons, rewards." The result is that "the Christian God looks like a great landowner administering his estates, the world" (HE,91). The Christian ideal is left without making any intrinsic sense of itself—such as is found in "physical relationships and organic connections." Everything is explained as "juridical relationships and moral attachments" which are revealed on faith and wholly apart from experience. Teilhard would argue that this is not really in keeping with the New Testament; "for St. John and St. Paul in particular, Christianity was essentially a cosmogony"

(W,250). Teilhard would allow that the language of the Gospels is "inclined to describe the Kingdom of God in terms of family or society," but he would argue that before the rise of modern science "the Incarnation could only find symbols of a juridical nature" (HE,91;C,68). Today such symbols appear "neolithic" and are judged to be of no further value. "The time is past in which God could simply impose himself on us from without as master and owner of the estate. Henceforth the world will only kneel before the organic center of its evolution."

The two rival stars could be identified as an *experience* of the world and as a *faith* in revelation. They involve different types of knowledge. In wanting to bring them together Teilhard is aware of various attempts at "concordism" wherein details from the Bible and data from scientific discoveries were artificially coordinated. He would claim that centuries of controversy have led all people to see that neither Science nor Revelation can be expected to do the work of the other; Science synthesizes experience, while Revelation involves a personal God who can be known only if he chooses to reveal himself.

The best way that the two rival stars could be identified is as *Totality* and *Personality*. Their properties oppose: one is "pantheist in tendency," while the other is personal. One is immanent and the other is transcendent; one has "organicity" and the other has "juridical relationships"; one is "evolutionary" and the other has "immutability" (S,120). But basically one is Totality and the other is a Person. Obviously the only way of reconciling these two would be if the Totality of the universe would become a Person. This is precisely the reconciliation that Teilhard envisions: "a god who makes himself cosmic and an evolution which makes itself a person (AE,381).

Descending in Order to Ascend

Teilhard frequently quotes a passage from St. Paul's Letter to the Ephesians (T,73,98,106;D,62,122,125;S,32,64;Lf,26;seeP,294) wherein Paul interprets a passage from Psalm 68 that speaks of the Lord ascending:

> In saying, "He ascended," what does it mean but that he (Christ) had also descended into the lower parts of the earth? He who descended is he who also ascended far above all the heavens, that he might fill all things (Eph.4:10–11).

This descent into the lower parts of the earth is what Teilhard will term the first part of a divine cycle. He tells of it in many ways: "the power of the Word Incarnate penetrates matter itself; it goes down into the deepest depths of the lower forces" (D,61–62); "in order to create . . . God has inevitably to immerse himself in the multiple, so that he may incorporate it in Himself" (T,196); "in order to bring all things back to the Father . . . he had to enter into contact with everyone of the zones of the created, from the lowest and most earthly to the zone that is closest to heaven" (C,71); "after sinking down to the depths of the earth, he has reached up to the heavens" (S,64). Thus Teilhard's basic theology of the Incarnation would see God entering matter at the first moment of creation at its lowest part. Only by descending to the basis of the earth at Alpha can he fill all things at Omega. One of the two stars, the transcendent God, has descended into the heart of the other, "immersing himself in things, by becoming 'element' " and then ascending from there to fill the totality. This is God's "kenosis" into matter; he has "inoculated" himself into the lowest part of the earth:

> Nothing can be absorbed into things except through the road of matter, by ascent from plurality. For Christ to make his way into the world by any side-road would be incomprehensible. The Redeemer could penetrate the stuff of the Cosmos, could pour himself into the life-blood of the universe, only by first dissolving himself in matter, later to be reborn from it (S,60).

The revealed Lord enters matter at its lowest level in order that He might rise from there to fill all things, *amictus mundi,* clothed in the glories of the world (D,61,128).

God comes to man through a descent in order to ascend—and this is also man's way to God. Thus the "divine cycle" is also a "natural cycle." It sends man "down to the bowels of matter in its full multiplicity, thence to climb back to the center of spiritual unification" (S,36). "On the model of the Incarnate God . . . I can be saved only by becoming one with the universe" (C,128). Thus, the Communion with God through matter. Matter is the principle of otherness. In entering matter both God and man become other than what they are. Through matter God and man can meet. God is not found through opposition to matter (anti-matter) or independent of matter (extra-matter) but through matter (trans-matter).

Union "must be effected by passing through and emerging from matter" (F, 106).

One can sense the significance of *"through-*matter" in the spirituality of Teilhard by a certain frequency of terms in his vocabulary derived from the Latin word, *trans*. He often called evolution "transformism"; species in transit transmit life giving rise to transitional forms. Matter is transient; rocks and men undergo transfigurations and transformations (and their Greek equivalent, metamorphoses) to become trans-human and trans-Christian and meet the trans-Christ. Fascinated by transparent rocks, Teilhard spoke of the translucency of Mary and of people becoming transparent to one another. Sin is a transgression. The transcendent God becomes transparent in the universe and the Transfiguration is seen as "perhaps the most beautiful mystery of the Christian faith" (UP, DesClausis, 6/Aug/46).

A "trans-matter" spirituality can be understood in the obvious sense to mean that we must use our material bodies or that we generally think in terms of images drawn from matter. But beyond such meanings Teilhard is saying we must pass through the *object known* and thus break down the radical separation generally assumed between the subject and object in any act of knowledge. The objective world is commonly presented as being on one side and man the observer is on the other: "things are projected for us 'just as they are' on a screen where we look at them without being mixed up in them" (HE, 113). But for Teilhard such a view can no longer be maintained; modern physics has shown us that the observer is inevitably part of what he observes, and modern biology has shown an evolving consciousness is studying its own evolution. The ideal of pure objectivity is no longer tenable; we can no longer flatter ourselves that we can regard the universe "from the outside 'like gods' " (HE, 114). It is this godlike regard that must descend and experience itself as part of a total process. This descent from subjectivity is what gives rise to the Cosmic Sense and it is what characterizes the mystic.

One of Teilhard's wartime writings ("The Mystical Milieu") enumerates a sequence of steps that tell of a "trans-matter" spirituality involving the cycle of descent and re-ascent. Teilhard begins by telling how fleeting sense experiences sometimes have taken possession of him and borne him away: "the world itself had invaded my being and had drawn me back into itself." The subject seems to merge with the object, "I felt my body, my soul, and even my spirit pass into the ethereal tint"; "when the world reveals itself to us, it draws us to itself; it causes us to flow outward." He enters an "homogeneous milieu" in which all differences "yearn to be melted away." Though it is called a phase of perception it involves an identification with the world not generally found in knowledge. The effect of the experience is "to break up our autonomy." This is the autonomy of the "pure" observer who wants to take an objective view, looking down on the universe like a god (the subject is not a part of the object). Now the seer finds "the mystical effort to see must give way to the effort to feel (*sentir*) and surrender myself. This is the phase of communion" (W,125). He allows his consciousness to become "wide as the skies and the earth . . . as deep as the past . . . as tenuous as the atom." He has descended into the lower parts, it is the basic experience of the mystical life, the Cosmic Sense. Teilhard surrenders himself in an act of communion and acknowledges that to many observers he would seem to be worshipping nature—for he has made the outward gesture of the pagan.

Having been drawn out of himself he found, "a new energy penetrated into me—or emerged from me, which I cannot say—that made me feel as vast and as loaded with richness as the universe." The energy that invades him is deeper than "the superficial autonomy of the soul." He is carried ever deeper into an ocean of energy and feels "creative energy flowing like sap into his life." He is now in "a homogeneous Milieu in which contrasts and differences are toned down." And his soul seeks not to be "distinguishable from the clear and vibrant milieu into which it sinks" (W,135). Then the phase of ascent begins: "The force that had been drawing the mystic towards the zone in which all things are fused together, now reverses its direction and brings him back to an exact examination of the experiential multiple" (W,136). The descent has meant that his own individual autonomy has (at least) partially dissolved, and other autonomies have done the same: "contrasts and differences are toned down." But with the ascent the mystic dedicates himself to the task of building God's kingdom on earth. Now he dedicates himself to human labor and strives to produce a result, an *opus*. In the homogeneous, all things were known as one; now by working he strives to make a *difference* by what he does. Now he is in the "cycle of the heterogeneous." Things are again defined—this is the ascent. Through the very process of his striving he begins to feel a mysterious presence, some other is emerging in

him "who is some part of ourselves, yet who masters us." Teilhard labors
to develop this immanent god, and then is passive as the transcendent
God bestows his fire upon the work. The mysterious presence assumes a
name and a face, it is Someone. But only the person himself can reveal
who he is. It is Jesus.

Teilhard gives a brief résumé of the stages through which he has passed:
it all began at a point and that point was his own autonomous person. The
point expanded as though it would absorb all things. Soon the point
became aware that it was not absorbing; it was being absorbed in a higher
unity that is gathering the universe into a new order. Everything is
centering around another point, around another person; he repeats the
other's name, Jesus, Jesus.

The effect of the process is termed a *transform*ation, for what is involved
is a change of form. In descending into the homogeneous milieu his own
form is (partially) lost; his soul seeks not to be "distinguishable from
the . . . milieu into which it sinks." It is from this more or less formless
state that he can rise to assume a new form: the Form of Christ. Matter is
essential for the process. Formally we are radically distinct from God.
Form (or essence) defines and sets apart, while matter allows diverse forms
to be part of one interacting world. If form were all we are, there would be
no possibility of union with God or with anything else. We would be as
separate as the formal categories of logic. It is through our matter that
others affect us. Through matter we are never wholly "what" we are. All
material things partially escape their defining form and thus can become
other. Matter makes beings "capable of unification" (W,267). In itself
matter does not unify, but it is that "through which the multitudinous
monads are bound together" (HU,69). It is through matter that we enter
the world and the world enters us. "By matter we are nourished, lifted up,
linked to everything else, invaded by life" (D,106). "Through matter" we
share in the entire history of life (D,57). My spirit partially animates and
partially effects the matter of the entire universe, and the spirits of all
other people partially animate and effect the same matter. Because of
matter all things are partially in my control and partially escape my
control. Through my matter others have the power to change my life;
through my matter I am vulnerable; through my matter I do not have the
autonomy I might desire. But matter is also that which enables me to
escape myself and enter into a wider world—or is it into nothingness?
Matter is ambiguous, it awakens both fear and fascination. I am drawn

"down to the bowels of matter in its full multiplicity" (S,56). But perhaps in faith I believe this is where I will meet my God, for He has descended into the lowest parts of the earth. Matter becomes my way of salvation, "I can only be saved by becoming one with the universe" (C,128). Like the bread that is eaten and loses its form as bread in order to be transformed into the one who has consumed it, so I must descend into a somewhat formless matter in order to be transformed into the Christ who has also descended there in order to rise, filling all things (see S,63,58). This is the "trans-matter" spirituality of Teilhard.

Teilhard presents this cycle of descent and ascent in many different contexts. In 1934 he was asked to write an account of his own faith; he responded with an essay ("How I Believe") that begins with an outline:

> In a first phase I feel the need to descend, step by step, to ever more elementary beliefs, until I can reach a certain fundamental intuition below which I can no longer distinguish anything at all. In a second phase, I try to ascend the natural series (. . .) of my successive acts of faith in the direction of an over-all view which ultimately is found to coincide with Christianity (C,99).

A similar sequence can be found in *The Phenomenon of Man;* there Teilhard begins with a descent to elemental matter only to find the "substratum of the tangible universe is in an unending state of disintegration as it goes downward" (P,41). Then Teilhard reverses direction to consider the upward movement of life as it works toward completing its "evolutionary cycle" (P,251). He ends with the Christian revelation.

Descent and ascent can be seen in the whole development of science since the Renaissance. Science turned away from the star of *faith* to that of *experience.* Astronomy showed the extent of the universe, and man seemed to be "engulfed in the enormous anonymity of the stellar bodies"; biology showed evolution, and man "vanished in the crowd of his fellow- species"; psychology told of the unconscious and man saw "an abyss of unconsciousness opened in the center of his I." Thus science had "projected the center of the world downwards." Its mysticism had "strayed off into the worship of matter" (HE,172). But Teilhard would see this movement as recently reversed (relativity shows the importance of the observer, etc.); "paradoxically . . . man is in process of re-emerging from his return to the crucible" (AM,268). The descent to the crucible is in the basic scientific process of analysis. Analysis proceeds "in a manner of speaking, *downwards."* But then, "starting from the lowest term at which it arrives, let us try, *moving upwards,* to appreciate the work of synthesis" (V,158).

In 1921 Teilhard gave a lecture in which the two directions are suggested in both the title and subtitle: *Science and Christ,* or *Analysis and Synthesis.* He sets out two propositions that he will defend: 1. Because the scientific study of the world is analytical, at first it makes us follow a direction that leads away from divine realities. 2. On the other hand, since this same scientific insight into things shows us the *synthetic structure* of the world, it obliges us to reverse our direction and, by its natural extension, turns us back to the unique center of things, which is God our Lord (S,21–22).

Analysis eventually shows us that there is no indivisible "atom" given in science, but "we had to get down to 'atoms' in order to realize this truth" (S,29). We then reverse direction and seek instead a synthetic unity by forming more comprehensive understandings and so approach God. But we can do this only after we have made the descent.

The descent and ascent recounted here coincide with the "reversal" outlined in "Cosmic Life" (see Chapter One of this study). But in "Cosmic Life" Teilhard thought that the descent was a mistake ("I had gone completely astray"). Now the descent is not a mistake but rather the analytic movement that is integral to science and a necessary part of the whole process—even though it takes us in "a direction that leads away from divine realities." The descent is part of the scientific process, without it we cannot ascend; "we had to get down to 'atoms' in order to realize this truth." A risk is involved, for the scientists who made these studies of matter "the temptation to surrender to it must have been very strong" (HE,172). Again, the Temptation of Matter! But now this temptation is the first and necessary phase of a cycle. Teilhard seems to lead us into temptation!

This descent and its temptation occur in areas more evidently moral. Teilhard allows that though it might generally be reprehensible to stoop "to certain sights and pleasures and doubts," this might be precisely what our soul needs for its nourishment (S,76–77). Christian teachers are seen to have erred in presenting a morality wherein the better course is identified with the safer course:

> Avoiding the risk of transgression has become more important to us than carrying a difficult position for God. And it is this that is

killing us. 'The more dangerous a thing, the more is its conquest ordained by life': it is from that conviction that the modern world has emerged; and from that our religion, too, must be reborn (T,75).

Matter remains a temptation, but science has faced it in order to give birth to the modern world; Christianity should now do the same. Danger is involved, but danger is a sign that great power is there: "Only a mountain can create a terrifying drop." Teilhard lived with danger at the front lines of World War I and there he found war fascinating and exhilarating. It kindled light in his soul, he claimed the very air was nourishing. The new life he discovered at the Front was "consecrated by danger" (HM,173–77). The need for danger or temptation is a sensitive issue: it concerns the descent "away from divine realities" and the outward gesture of the pagan. Some of the passages on danger were written as part of a reflection on his own strong feelings for women. Women were a danger to his vow of celibacy, but he did not believe that he should simply turn away from them for in the presence of the danger he found life; his spirit was *nourished* by their company—but his spirit also retained something else: a commitment made to the revealed God.

When Teilhard first spoke of the two foci (stars), the first was identified with experience and the second with revelation (see first page of this chapter). Accordingly the two "foci-stars" are part of him in very different ways: there is an "innate cosmic sense" by which I experience the All, while the Christic sense is "by education": one is a *"gout naif"* while the other is a *"gout transmis"* ("sucked in with my mother's milk"—HM,41–42); one is the "discovered" and the other is the "taught" (AE,404); one is there by temperament and the other is there by upbringing (C,96). His response to the two is likewise different: to the All he responds with passion: "cosmic passion" (J,124); "passion for the world" (C,130); "the passionate awareness of the universal quasi presence" (T,202); "the only primordial, irrepressibly ebullient passion in the human heart" (W,121); "the most fundamental form of passion" (P,261). "We have but one passion: to become one with the world that envelops us without ever being able to distinguish either its face or its heart" (C,58). Without distinguishing face or heart! Thus the passion for the All is radically impersonal; it is a "unique, consuming passion" that can draw man away from the people he loves (HU,67). And underneath the passion a man feels for a woman, lies "a passion intended for the All" (HE,34).

But Teilhard's involvement with the opposite star-focus (the revealed God of whom he has been taught) is not a passion (see however, C,156;Li,137). Here Teilhard judges "a good intention as the necessary start and foundation of all else," "purity of intention," "the pure heart, the right intention," the "moral value if intention" (D,53,65,121,133; W,53,211,258;C,72;HM,216;J,64,310,312). What is significant now is not an innate and passionate drive but the reflective orientation that one gives himself as a moral person; "through the pure intent of my will the divine must flood into the universe" (W,126). The intention or intent towards the second star gives one a certain tension, while the call of matter is to relax the inner tension (W,32). Thus the appeals of the two stars could be contrasted: "The one involves relaxation and expansion, the other tension and centration" (AE,219).

The intention or intent to Christ is the direction the Christian gives his will, but with this there can often be a limitation in that the intent can become hollow or empty if it is divorced from the deep, instinctive movement of the soul—from one's roots in the earth—from the "primordial, irrepressibly ebullient passion" for the All. Thus many Christians have a reflective commitment (right intention) but lead an artificial life in that they lack "the bread of earthly things to nourish them, the wine of created beauties to intoxicate them" and soon end up with "feeble powers and bloodless hearts" (D,106). Christian spirituality is in danger of becoming lost in the clouds "unless it receives a new blood transfusion from matter" (T,128). Christians have been condemned by Marxists as being removed from the concerns of the earth; Christianity seems to set them apart "instead of merging them with the mass" (D,68). The Christian needs a return to matter, to mass, to an expansion of his being, to a risk—lest his reflective commitment set him apart from his fellow men and the world of experience. The *personal intent* should not leave him estranged from his *impersonal passion* for the All.

Teilhard would urge that to rejuvenate our *supernatural* forces we must drive "roots deep into the nutritious energies of the earth." This is the descent. But since one has a reflective commitment he does not make this descent the same way that the pagan, pantheist or Buddhist would. Rather, the individual makes only "the outward gesture of the pagan," "the same gesture as the Buddhist," "exactly the same appearances" (D,119;Li,246;W,113,126). Both the pagan and the Christian love the world: the pagan to confine himself or herself within it; the Christian to make it purer and draw from it the strength to escape. The pagan and the Christian are both involved in the world: the pagan for his or her own delight and the Christian to bring the world's energies back to God. The outward appearance is the same, but the Christian retains the other star: an intent, "He pre-adheres to God" (D,119). Much of Teilhard's descent was concerned with his field work in geology (back to the roots in matter, etc.). He would term geology "part of the total gesture of my life" but "by itself of no ultimate interest" (LT,86). The work is only a gesture because the intent of his will remains fixed: he did his geologic research with the intent "of being better able to speak of the 'great Christ' " (LT,88).

The descent that Teilhard made into Nirvana in the beginning of "Cosmic Life" could also be described as a gesture. Though he tells of making an "experiment" with "no holding back," he couches the passage in phrases like "perhaps" and "I may well have." One can well object that if it was an "experiment," there was indeed something held back. He further states that he moved *"towards Nirvana"*—which is not the same as arriving, otherwise it would have been difficult to reverse. What he was holding back was the intent of his will, the other star by which he "pre-adhered" to God. Many Zen masters would regard any pre-adherence as an obstacle to Nirvana, Nirvana should be free of all intents. But even a partial descent involves some danger.

Matter is a temptation; Nirvana is a temptation; woman is a temptation. The temptation is for one to renounce the pre-adherence by which his life has purpose—that is what all temptation is. But, beyond the pre-adherence, the soul must take some risks, for it needs the nourishment of matter (science), of Nirvana (the Cosmic Sense!), and of woman. When he first began writing, Teilhard saw that "The salvation of the soul must be bought at the price of a great risk incurred and accepted" (W,113). Shortly before his death he would write, "Even today I am still learning by experience the dangers" of the path. "I still tremble often, even as I pursue it" (HM,46–47).

When St. Paul spoke of the Lord descending "into the lowest part of the earth," he spoke also of a descent made with an intent: to ascend "that he might fill all things." Thus the Incarnation involved an intent with some holding back. Teilhard speaks of God "Partially immersing himself in things" (P,294). (Teilhard sees this possible since God is triune Li,274.)

Teilhard would term the entrance of God into the world a baptism. This would again suggest a descent and an ascent:

> Christ immerses himself in the waters of the Jordan, symbol of the forces of the earth. These he sanctified. And as he emerges, in the words of St. Gregory of Nyssa, with the waters which run off his body he elevates the whole world (D,110).

In the divine descent the two stars come together, the divine Person immerses himself in the Totality. The human person must go to meet him there, and this is also a baptism:

> The movement carried out by the man who plunges into the world, in order first to share in things and then to carry them along with him . . . is an exact replica of the baptismal act (T,73).

This movement is our "baptism into cosmic matter" (S,58). Those with an intent towards God must also undergo a "baptism of fire." Priests sent to the battle lines in World War I had "a baptism into reality" (MM,26). The heavenly Jerusalem itself will wither "without its baptism" (D,154) into matter. Baptism is the meeting of the two stars; thus the term is often applied to the rising Totality as it receives the descending Christ. The soul of the world must be baptized (Li,143); the energies of the earth must be baptized (S,120); "neo-humanism" must be baptized (UP, Martindale,11/Dec/48); the "tendency to pantheism" must be baptized (W,207); Communism must be baptized (Li,255). Or, changing the word slightly, the collectivization of the earth must be "christened" (LT,282); the tendency to pantheism is what "we must *explicitly Christianize*" (W,189). We must feel the heart of the earth beating within us "as we Christianize it" (D,154). In each baptism the Christ is formed. For by each baptism God is again immersed into matter and matter is again elevated into God. Matter is "Christened."

Since Teilhard urges that we must "explicitly Christianize" the world, he would probably have some difficulty with the way some use the phrase "anonymous Christian." Not that Teilhard disregarded Christian elements in other religious traditions; he often expressed appreciation of them. But the fullness of Christianity is present only when the anonymous and impersonal striving of the earth gain the *name* and *face* of Christ. "The essential of Christianity (is) . . . to positively place the world in relation with the Supreme Personal, that is to say, to name Him" (Li, 309). Teilhard saw that his vocation among scientists was "to personalize the world in God" (LT, 222). Teilhard would tell of climbing a plateau in central China; "standing there, I offered the world of Mongolia to Christ, whose name no man has ever invoked in that place" (LT, 119). Thus it is through our explicit Christian intent that the world is Christianized in us; its anonymous and impersonal strivings take on a heart and a face. Baptism is the act of Christianization, it is the act whereby the two stars come together and the Christ is formed. The foci come together; the All enters the Divine Person and the Divine Person fills all things.

Two Stars and Three Elements

Though Teilhard often wrote of the two stars and their attractions, he also often wrote of three elements and two of the three seem to resemble the two stars. Thus, he describes himself as "a curious blend of Hindu 'totality,' Western 'technology,' and Christian 'personalism' " (LTF, 113). Taking the same three elements he would divide his spiritual autobiography in three parts according to "three universal components: the Cosmic, the Human, and the Christic" (HM, 15). These would be expressed as differing shades within his soul: "the Crimson of Matter," "the Gold of Spirit," and "the Incandescence of Some One" (HM, 50). He would even present these three in an ascending sequence:

> Crimson gleams of Matter, gliding imperceptibly into the gold of Spirit, ultimately to become transformed into the incandescence of a Universe that is Person (HM, 16).

Corresponding to these shades of soul there are three sectors in the world today: "the Eastern (or Hindu) quarter," "the Marxist quarter," and "the Christian quarter" (AE, 224–25). Thus humanity is left with "three basic options:" the Eastern current, Faith in Man, and Western Christianity (S, 253).

These same three elements are treated at length in *How I Believe*. Here they are three religious alternatives that present themselves in the world of today: "the group of Eastern religions, the humanist neopantheisms, and Christianity" (C, 121). Teilhard considers each in turn: Eastern religions appeal because they are "supremely universalist and cosmic." They began in a form of pantheism that flowered in India centuries ago. He claims to be particularly sensitive to Eastern influences, but in coming to understand them better he saw that they spoke of an "homogeneous unity in which the complete adept is lost to self, all individual features and values being suppressed." Thus he tells of turning from the venerable horizons of Asia to the other end of the horizon and to the youthful forms of religion born in the West: the humanist neopantheisms. These—apart from their Marxist form—are as yet hardly codified. They offer no apparent God; but Teilhard would still call them religions as they involve a contagious faith in an ideal: one devotes "oneself body and soul to a universal progress." Together they form the "religion of evolution." In this religion Teilhard would see many of the values he has been seeking: it has a vibrant spirit; it promotes research; and it strives for the greater development of human consciousness. But once again Teilhard finds limitations in this religion: those who dedicate themselves to advancing a common world spirit have no way of justifying their dedication unless the spirit they advance were "endowed with immortality and personality" (C,124). Many of those who work for human progress refuse even to discuss the possibility of immortality; Teilhard finds this limitation stifling. He then turns his attention to Christianity, and Christianity is identified as the religion of personality and immortality. But in spite of these advantages Teilhard finds the Christianity presented today to be constrained by a juridical and extrinsicist vocabulary.

To avoid the weakness in each position Teilhard proposes a unity of the three religious currents in a religion of the universal Christ; this is a synthesis of the universe, progress, and the transcendent God. Now in Christ his "deepest pantheist aspirations are satisfied, guided and reassured" (C,128). He foresees an eventual convergence of these three currents:

> In the great river of mankind, the three currents (Eastern, human and Christian) are still at crosspurposes. Nevertheless there are sure indications which make it clear that they are coming to run together. (C,130).

The whole sequence sounds familiar, but now there are three elements, not two. The three converging currents could be identified as the All, the Becoming, and a Person. The three coming together would form the universal Christ and from the three terms the thought of Teilhard could be summarized in three words: *All Becoming Christ.* Then the two stars could be seen as the first and third of the three elements, while the second element is the process by which the first proceeds to the third. The process has only recently been revealed through the advance of modern science and a corresponding sense of an evolving cosmos. Thus, for centuries pantheism was considered incompatible with the Christ of the Gospels, but now with the advances of Western science the image of a static universe is rejected and people now sense a universal Becoming. Until science showed all of matter in a vast process of rising to Spirit, the full implications of St. Paul could not be understood. Now man's pantheistic urges are seen to be integral to a complete Christianity. Thus Teilhard would speak of evolution as holy, for it is the process by which the All advances into the transcendent Person of God.

The three elements run through the writings of Teilhard and the best way of considering them would be to schematize them in three parallel columns:

All	Becomong	Person	
Eastern Totality	Western Technology	Christian Personalism	LFT,113
Eastern religions, Nirvana	Humanist, Marxist, Building the Earth	Christianity	C,121&ff.
Crimson of Matter	Gold of Spirit	Incandescence of Some One	HM,16,50
Matter	Spirit	Divine Reality	HU,50
Close eyes & disappear	Humanistic religion	Christian religion	D,43,45
Matter	Soul	Christ	D,62
Matter	Spirit	Christ	HM,216
Cosmos (unconscious)	Life-Mankind	God	HM,212
Matter of Matter, Rock	Spirit (true matter), Mind	Soul of Souls Form of forms	HM,21;W, 168,275
Non-Being	Becoming	Being	
Past (roots)	Present	Future	
Terminus a quo	Evolution	*Terminus ad quem*	
Will of God	God's creative action	God's formal influx	W,294ff.

Experience, the All, Universalism	Futurism	Faith, revelation, Personalism	LT,225,228
East	Movement West	West	
Potency	Actualization	Act	
Potentia	*Operatio*	*Opus*	
Passion, Cosmic Sense, nourishment, relaxation	Sublimation, synthesizing	Intent tension	
Spheric (Hindu)	Cosmogenesis	Centric	J,23/Dec/54
Periphery (homogenous)	Current (living)	Divine Center	J,171
Science	Act of knowledge	Religion	P,285
Research	Evolution	Adoration	J,29/Jul/53
Analysis	Synthesizing	Final synthesis	

The three columns can serve as a structure in order to see parallels in the thought of Teilhard. First, there is the sequence Teilhard knew in his own development from "Crimson to Gold to Incandescence." There is also the sequence from fascination with rocks as a child at Sarcenat, to evolution as a student in Sussex, to *Forma Christi* as a soldier in the trenches of World War I. The three columns also present the sequence he went through in his sense for God (see Chapter One): first the Divine Will (identified with Matter [J,28], and nourishment [D,121]), then God's creative action, and finally the formal influx of God. The columns also show the three terms from the "verses" presented in Chapter One: "Everything in the Cosmos is for Spirit," the natural verset; "Everything in Spirit is for Christ," the supernatural verset. The sequence also shows the continuity Teilhard saw between the natural and supernatural. (The same natural-supernatural sequence is present in the complex "syllogism" in the first part of *The Divine Milieu;* the three terms of the syllogism are matter, soul and God, D,56–62.)

The columns also pick up the training of the vision presented in Chapter Two: the humano-cosmic phenomenon (columns two and one) had to be completed to become the divine-humano-cosmic phenomenon. In each case the middle term is the process by which the first term rises towards the third. But before one can rise to the third one must descend to the first: one must do analysis before one can rise to the final synthesis; one must do research to rise in adoration; the pursuit of science gives rise to religion. Science and Religion are movements in opposite directions, but they are not opposed; they are "the two conjugated faces or phases of one and the same complete act of knowledge" (P,285).

Teilhard first made his own descent when fragments of iron and rock disintegrated; he lost all love for the particular and turned to the universal "Stuff of Things." This was the descent. In 1905 he went to Egypt and there "the East" flooded over him in "a wave of the exotic" (HM,23). He would do his first excavation there and later go to the Far East to do most of his digging in the earth. He developed a geographical bias according to which going East symbolized his descent into matter: "a voyage to the Far East represents a sort of 'temptation of the multiple' " (Li,104). He went East seeking "the fermenting mass of the peoples of Asia" and "currents of mysticism in process of formation" (LT,100). Asia was as much characterized by sleep and "absence of thought" (LT,100–102), as he had previously found Nirvana (Eastern religion) to be characterized by the "silence of sleep" and "a lack of thought" (W,30,66). The people were "extremely earthbound"; they "slumber embedded in that lower zone" (LLZ,65,53). Asia was where he sought the primordial origin of man; Nirvana was "primordial" and "origin." In Asia he worked in the crumbling wastes of the Gobi desert, in Nirvana he found endless disintegration. Going to Asia was his descent: "What force impels me, once more, towards Asia? Only a wind blowing from our present life back over the abyss of the past." But working there he found "the tide of consciousness whose waves carried me towards the past is beginning to turn" (V,184). The Orient should be seen "at dusk when the sun bearing the spoils of Asia with it in its glory, rises in triumph over the skies of Europe" (LT,103). He had descended with a purpose: "I only came to China in the hope of being better able to speak about the 'great Christ' in Paris" (LT,88).

Perhaps the appropriateness of the parallels could be seen by considering the descent as presented in "Cosmic Life"; there the three columns are implicit and many of the elements within each column are associated: When he makes the descent he finds "the *eastern* vision," "instinct with *passion*," "*from* which" all has emerged, for the "*Hindu* . . . all is *materialized*." One attains a "primordial consciousness . . . ever more *relaxed*," for the benefit "of the rudimentary and *diffuse* forms of being."

When Teilhard "reverses" he moves to the second column: he reversed because of a "faith in *life*," in "a direction of *growth* . . . a *progress* in consciousness," a "belief in human *progress*"; he will " 'work' as though with a *leaven*," for "cosmic *development*" and "the absolute *evolution* of Being." When he sees that non-Christian humanists are limited in that they "can only look to a *Becoming*," he moves to the third column. Here he finds "the *object* of every process" in the *revealed Christ;* the Christian can speak personally to "Him who *is*."

Each time that Teilhard tells of a descent to the lower parts of the earth, what he encounters is potentiality. He would compare it with Aristotle's prime matter; it is pure possibility. Matter is an "inexhaustible potentiality for existence" (HU,69); there are "rich potentialities hidden in Matter" (W,33), and the universe is termed "a vast resevoir of potencies" (T,69). Christ is seeking out "the world's potentialities" (D,154), and it is by actualizing them through human work that Christ will attain his fulfillment. Sometimes Teilhard wrote as though potentialities, potential, and energy were the same (AE,390). Thus at the base of his descent he meets "formless energy to which the pantheisms of the inanimate try to cling" (HE,142); "energy, the prime multiform stuff of all phenomena" (HE,361); "energy—that floating universal entity . . . the new God . . . the Impersonal" (P,258). The cosmic sense itself is a type of energy (AE,219). The final level of the mystics' descent is the "Circle of Energy"; there the energies are defined as "transient activities" and monads "linked together by transient forces." The descent that begins *The Phenomenon of Man* encounters energy as a "kind of homogeneous promordial flux," "a capacity . . . for interaction" (P,42). Contact with the earth always brought Teilhard new energies: "I regained a burst of life from contact with Africa's soil" (UP, LeMaitre, 2/March/55); "I continue to feel the helpful excitation of this new contact with the terrain" (UP, Mortier,10/Sep/51), "The first delight of exploring the past isthe refreshment it brings to our minds" (V,185); "This plunge in the grand geological and biological realities (the Origins of Man and the Continents) has refreshed me. The spiritual power of Matter!" (Li,388).

These energies are the nourishment of his soul—but they must be given a direction. Throughout the long ages of life this direction has been instinctive, and Teilhard tells of a secular scientist who continued to work because of "his instinctive taste" (LLZ,49). But as man becomes increasingly reflective Teilhard did not believe this instinctive motivation would be sufficient. It is when the world of human progress reflects on its goals that it must turn to the transcendent world: to religion.

Thus the one star of undefined Energy needs the influence of the other star, the revealed Word, in order to continue its growth. The energy of the world has become partially personalized in man; now only a deeply personal call will enable the potentiality of the cosmos to be fully actualized. The Mankind of today constitutes the rising tide of Totality; Man stirs with a cosmic passion. But also, in a way that often puzzles him, a way that seems to conflict with his Cosmic Sense, man is aware of the transcendent, the Person, the Christ awaiting his completion. These are the two stars, they are the first and the third elements presented in the columns above; they are the two foci of the human soul. But there is also the second column, the Becoming, the middle term that links the two. The Becoming is Man, that is, the soul that has two foci. The Becoming is the rising Spirit of Earth; it is ourselves; "we are evolution" (P,232). We are the process rising on a tide of technology and research. We are the act of knowing with one face towards research and the other towards adoration. Through research "the world has entered our soul." But the world will not stop there; it seeks a height above the human soul. The soul is only the place of passage. In the Introduction to this study a poem was quoted that well expressed the situation:

> All things search until they find
> God through the gateway of thy mind.

We are the gateway through which the rising All is reaching for God. One of the foci-stars of our soul is the risen Christ summoning the universe into himself. The other focus-star (the geometry of the image becomes difficult) is likened to the surface of a sphere; the Totality is spread out. By our descent into the Totality the energy of the universe enters us and through this entrance the Totality itself:

> seeks anxiously in the heart of each one of us for a universal centre of thought and affection. Here a sphere (Totality) calling for a centre. There a centre (Christ) awaiting a sphere. Far from contradicting one another, as might be feared, the two stars of totality and personality attract one another within the human soul . . . A conjunction is therefore inevitable. Now from this eventual conjunction will follow:

the total sap of things will break in a single heart; man will cherish
the world as a person and more than a person; a love will be born for
the first time on earth as great and strong as the universe (HE, 159).

Today Man bears within himself the Totality of the energies of the earth
and so he can turn to his God and say "that he loves Him with his whole
body and soul, and with the *whole universe*" (HE, 159; S, 172; HM, 101). He
can no longer see himself as a separate fragment, he is an "in-gathering" of
the earth brought to consciousness; so when he loves God he loves Him
"with every fibre of the unifying universe" (P, 297). In return "as through
a sacred door . . . God passes through him" into all things (W, 144). In
Man, once again, the two stars come into conjunction as the Christ is
formed in "an explosion of dazzling flashes." Man himself is the middle
term wherein the rising universe finds its God and the descending Person
of Christ is invested with the majesty of creation.

Chapter Four

ANOTHER THING LIVES IN HIM AND DOMINATES HIM
The Reflection of Subject and Object

Teilhard believed that both the cosmic and the Christic foci of his soul were with him since childhood. But it was during his military service that he first became aware of the connecting term, Humanity. At the Front he gained the "faculty of *perceiving*, without actually *seeing*, the reality and organicity of collective magnitudes"; Humanity became as real as a giant molecule of protein (HM,31). But, like other men, Teilhard recognized in himself a reluctance to become part of any "collective magnitude." Collective magnitudes seem to be a threat to our personal freedom and lead to fusion and unconsciousness. Each of us is aware of a "fine point of ourselves that comes up into the light of self-consciousness and freedom" (see D,75). We value highly our center of freedom. But this fine point can also be the center of our difficulties, for it seems to be precisely the element that sets us apart from one another and makes us wary of Humanity. It often seems that the more we develop and protect our personal identity, the more we confine ourselves to living in reflective isolation.[1]

The pinnacle of self-consciousness we have attained seems to render us solitary Titans. The urge for unity with our fellow man seems to require that we surrender our inwardness and merge in the human collectivity. We seem to be faced with two alternatives: either the increased loneliness of the reflective Titan, or the fusion with others in a collective Nirvana. Teilhard suggests a third possibility: Christ as the union in which reflective centers are differentiated. He sets together the three possibilities: "Nirvana (identification); Titans (aloneness, egoism); or Jesus (union)" (J,25/Mar./52, see also J,45,54).

The Subject of Action

Teilhard introduced an essay on the evolution of spirit by saying "this is what I believe I have seen—confronting the world alone" (HE,19). This sense of a solitary confrontation is suggested in many of his early essays; for example, consider the imaginative account of the desert traveler that was presented in Chapter Two. This man went "far from humanity's caravan routes" to "the untouched wilderness"; leaving "the wordiness of social life" he confronts Reality "entire and untamed." Another imaginative account tells of a seer who "leaves the public place and returns to the firm deep bosom of Nature" (F,24). Teilhard would see nobility in a solitary quest: those who have "never known the passion for new horizons" are not fully human. Those who have made the solitary venture are changed forever:

> Men who have suffered, even to the verge of death, from thirst or cold, can never again forget the deserts or the pack-ice where they enjoyed the intoxication of being the first and only men (HM,171).

But new horizons are also available to the thinker "whose mind rises up to difficult and unusual ways of looking at things." Teilhard was dazzled by what he saw alone; then he came "down from the mountain" to tell others about it. He wanted to leave aside his individualism and confront the general experience of mankind. But he is disconcerted to discover that there is not a single authority or book that tells of the same vision. He begins to doubt his experience and ask himself if he is only the plaything of a mirage in his own mind. It is only gradually that he finds confirmation but it appears all around him: when he tells others what he has seen his ideas are eagerly accepted. Soon his understanding begins to spread with a contagious quality among all kinds of people "from the border-line of unbelief to the depths of the cloister" (HM,101). It seems that other people already understood what he was about to say and were only waiting to hear it expressed. He finds so much support that soon he hesitates to call his ideas his own; his message is rather what Humanity itself is trying to express. Each time he meets another who has seen and feels as he, he finds he is drawn to that person and feels closer than a brother (AE,74). It is as if he and others like him were only "pieces of persons calling out for one another" (AE,118); they no longer perceive themselves as isolated fragments but as "elements of a single Spirit in search of itself" (F,95;HE,13). In any large gathering individuals who are "endowed with this 'mysterious' sense . . . will gravitate instinctively towards one another in the crowd, they will recognize one another" (F,143). Teilhard tells of having experienced this a hundred times. He finds himself drawn across social and religious barriers provided only that "the same flame of expectation burns in us both"; there is a "total contact instantly established" (F,143). Such individuals know that tomorrow "the whole world will see what they see and think as they do" (F,100).

Teilhard would believe each person must leave "humanity's caravan routes" and reflect alone in "the untouched wilderness," but in so doing one does not isolate oneself. It is that very experience of untouched wilderness that gives one a sense of the earth and "tends to break the disastrous isolation which envelops spiritual monads (men)" (HE,36). The ones who are really drawn together in social gathering are the bold adventurers, the explorers of new dimensions, those possessed by "the demon (or angel) of Research" (F,142). The rest of humanity are perhaps busy quarreling or amusing themselves; they are even puzzled by the explorer for they "sense his compulsion to be forever seeking something *behind themselves*" (HU,67). And what is "behind" each man or woman is *Humanity itself*. Humanity behind each individual, but *"Humanity grouped by the act of discovery"* (HE,171). Teilhard presents "a mysticism of discovery" (HE,171); thus it is to the bold "conquistadores" that Teilhard sees himself speaking, for by their adventure he is sure *they* have sensed a common Spirit.

Teilhard takes comfort that he is "not a lone discoverer" but only one who is particularly sensitive to vibrations everywhere about him. He begins to suspect that he has discovered nothing by himself; he is only the first to speak of what others have also come to know. The vision is not found in books of an earlier age, as it required the whole modern understanding of an evolving cosmos to make it possible. Teilhard has seen more only because he has stood in a privileged place, that is, he has been deeply involved in both the scientific and Christian milieu and has allowed the two influences to act on each other. He finds confirmation in the enthusiasm that his writings begin to generate:

It is, in consequence, exhilarating to feel that I am not just myself or all alone, that my name is legion, that I am "all men," and that this is true even as much as the unanimity of tomorrow recognizes itself throbbing in my depths (HM, 101; Translation amended: The French reads: *"se reconnait palpitante au fond de moi, l'unanimité de demain."*).

Teilhard admired Newman's *Apologia pro Vita Sua,* a highly personal account of Newman's own conversion. By writing a very personal account Newman's work had a universal appeal. Teilhard believed others should write such books: books that are so personal that their appeal is universal. When Teilhard writes a statement of his own faith he tells of "the developments of a personal experience" that is "set in completely subjective terms," but he is confident that such an account will be understood. If others will only look deeply within themselves, they will "find a common substratum" (C, 97). *In the depths of one's own person* one encounters not so much oneself as Humanity. This is his fundamental thesis when he writes of his own faith, so he sets it in italics: "It is through that which is most incommunicably personal in us that we make contact with the universal" (CE, 97–98).[2]

It is by speaking from the heart that we speak to the heart of all humanity. Our reflective centers do not isolate us as lonely "Titans"; rather it is through these centers and deeper than these centers that we contact a common spirit. Perhaps in certain valued moments we have sensed that it was not so much our own soul speaking as the spirit of Man speaking through us. On such an occasion the people before us understand what we say for we are giving them voice; "What is already thinking through man and above man is mankind" (AE, 38). Mankind is seeking expression. If we give it expression the people before us will understand, for we speak what they feel. Teilhard introduces an essay with the explanation:

a spiritual urge has been trying to express itself in me . . . I feel, indeed, that it is not I that conceived this essay: it is a man *(un Homme)* within me who is greater than I—a man whom I have recognized countless times, and always the same, close to me (S, 38).

In speaking of a Man within him, or Mankind within him, conceiving the essay that he himself writes, Teilhard introduces the ambiguities many creative people have encountered in identifying the subject of actions —the doer of deeds—one would ordinarily call his own. It seems a creative force from within takes over and acts for one. Teilhard wrote an imaginative account in which he tells of "taking the lamp" and, leaving the zone of everyday occupations and relationships where everything seems clear, going down to the abyss of his inmost self from which he feels dimly that his *"power of action emanates."* But as he moves further and further from the conventional certainties by which social life is superficially illuminated, he feels that he is losing contact *with himself.* At each step of the descent a new person is disclosed within him whose name he does not know and who does not obey him. He finally comes to a bottomless abyss, "and out of it came—arising I know not from where—the current which I dare to call *my* life" (D,77).

What Teilhard is saying can be set in the terminology of Freud: the ego discovers that it is no longer master in its own house. To explain himself Teilhard appeals to the findings of Freud and adds, "we find with horror that we are made of all sorts of fibres . . . fibres that come from every quarter and from very far afield, each with its own history and life—fibres that are always ready to escape from our control and unravel" (AE,188). The whole current of his life does not seem to belong to him, it was not he who set it in motion. Unfamiliar drives have urged him into acts that he never intended, many of these drives can be traced back to a bestial past, and then back beyond all traces. Teilhard becomes disturbed by what he has seen (so much "faceless matter") so he directs his attention back to the familiar world of social relationships and tries to forget the disturbing enigmas found within. But suddenly the spectres he had encountered within are waiting to devour him in the outside world. Now they are identified as *the web of chance,* the very stuff of which the whole universe is woven. Our mind is disturbed when it tries to plumb the depths of the fibres within us; it is said to reel even more when it tries to consider the favorable chances that must coincide at every moment if the least of our actions is to succeed (D,78). Our being born and the whole course ofour lives have depended on accidents over which we have had no control. Teilhard becomes dizzy as he considers the tremendous improbability of his ever existing—and the further improbability of there ever being a world that has survived. He feels the distress of a particle adrift in the universe floating through a crushing number of living things and stars.

Then in an obscure way he is saved—for he seems to be aware of the voice of Christ saying, "It is I, do not be afraid." He responds by a double act of trust: one hand of Christ is believed to run through the current that makes up the inner flow of his life, while the other hand of Christ runs through the seemingly chance events of all that happens in the world. It is Christ "in the life which wells up within me and in the matter which sustains me." Now he does not experience the inner and outer worlds as hostile, but as the two loving hands of God:

> one which holds us so firmly that it is merged, in us, with the sources of life, and the other whose embrace is so wide that, at its slightest pressure, all the springs of the universe respond harmoniously together (D,78–79).

When Teilhard began his inner journey he was seeking the source of his own power of *action*. But in the prayer which follows he asks only "to sketch the outline of a *gesture*." He does not so much act as make a gesture. And the word, gesture, runs through the writings of Teilhard. He feels he can hardly call his "deeds" his own, for forces active long before he was born have entered into him and have given rise to "his" acts. And forces beyond his control will lead those acts to results he never intended: "We are in the grip of forces many millions of times transcending our individual liberties" (F,101). Teilhard discovers he is all but helpless over the course of events in which he will share. This helplessness could bring distress and a sense of defeat to the majority of people, but not to the mystic. It is the mystic's delight. St. Augustine had spoken of what is *"in nobis, sine nobis,"* within us without being us. Teilhard quotes him often (J,48,59;D,49;W,215;UP, Fontoynont,15/Mar/16). For the mystic the world would lose all of its savor and grandeur

> if he did not feel *so completely swept away* in the divine ocean that *no initial point of support* would be left him in the end, of his own, within himself, from which he could act (D,44).

The mystic has no point from which to act, so he or she only makes the gesture. Teilhard would refer to all of his life as a gesture. His work in China was a gesture, geology was a gesture, writing was a gesture, the witness of his faith was a gesture, to humanize and to Christify constitute a double gesture, and he prays to finish his life "in the best gesture for Christ's glory and revelation." Then he further limits his own role: "If I make 'the gesture' it is because Our Lord will make me make it" (Retreat,25/Oct/45). He is speaking of what he repeatedly found in experience, that: *he is not the doer of his deeds*. He would begin to write a personal statement of faith, but then add "as I proceeded I felt that something greater than myself was working its way into me" (C,130). He would stand amidst the rock piles of Asia and feel "sudden and brief fits of awareness of the laborious unification of things," and "it is no longer myself thinking, but the Earth acting." He found this to be "infinitely better" (LTF,73).

Teilhard is known for presenting a mysticism of action, but as is the case in numerous mysticisms, the mystic does not sense himself or herself to be the one acting. Teilhard would write "the subject is unquestionably no longer the human monad, but the world" (T,50). For Teilhard, action is found to have a whole series of subjects: sometimes it is the universe, sometimes it is matter, sometimes it is evolution, sometimes it is life, sometimes it is mankind and sometimes the subject is the two hands of God. In the course of evolution when diverse species began to appear on the tree of life, it was the *universe* which began to ramify (P,92). With the appearance of man it is "the stuff of the universe . . . becoming thinking" (P,251); in man "the universe has become conscious of itself," "the universe reflects itself" (HE,102;P,251). When people socialize "it is the entire universe which . . . animates itself" and ultimately it is "the universe fulfilling itself in a synthesis" (P,294). Man is "nothing else than evolution become conscious of itself . . . In each individual consciousness it is evolution perceiving itself and reflecting on itself" (P,221;translation amended).It is "self-reflective evolution" at work (MPN,120). Evolution must "effect through us a work of absolute value" (S,177); "evolution passes through the human personality without staying there" (HE,65). Man is "one of the cosmic stuff's innumerable attempts to involute on itself" (T,173). "Matter thinks itself" (J,22/Mar/52); "the stuff of the universe" becomes thinking (P,251).

Teilhard had said that the world has entered into our souls, and that is precisely what we find when we look there. What has occurred is an "enlarging of our separate personalities" (F,17). We come to see that it is "the universe, in one of its fundamental movements, that would emerge in our consciousness, and the universe battling deep down in our wills" (S,95). Previously people could not understand "the obscure urges which sometimes reach them in great waves from the deep places of the world"

(HE, 32). But now man sees himself differently, he is "hominized earth" or "hominized Nature." He is the Cosmos become thinking. Teilhard titled his first essay "Cosmic Life" for the cosmos itself is alive and acting in all of the living. Each "individual" is only a microcosm in which and through which the cosmos acts. The more nobly a man tries to act, the more he will find that he does not want to live for himself and the remunerative aspects of his work. He begins wanting new paths to blaze and new truths to discover for Mankind. Gradually he realizes that he no longer belongs to himself; "little by little the great breath of the universe has insinuated itself into him." Now it is this breath which raises him up and bears him along. (D, 72; S, 70). This breath is the delight of the mystic. By his deeds he comes to discover that he is not the doer; they are being done by that strange Other that is *in nobis, sine nobis.*

Teilhard first became aware of this higher Presence while he was at the Front. He claimed it is "instilled into us by the immanence of an extreme common danger"; in such moments we are "admitted to the miracle of a common soul." But he would add, it comes "for awhile" (W, 286). The breaths of higher consciousness pass away; they are "more intermittent" than one's personal consciousness (C, 53). When they were absent Teilhard would tell of a "nervous weakness that paralyzes me in everything" (LTF, 105). He would sink into a despondency in which he lost all will to live; he could not act himself, he could only "pray . . . until the current of activity reestablished itself" (J, 84). It would seem that this paralysis was the price he had to pay for knowing the exaltation of the marvellous Other within himself as the Doer. When its "more intermittent" presence was gone, he was overcome by a great lassitude in which he was unwilling or unable to act at all. He claimed that whatever forces or ardors he might have:

> are not me, but deeper than me, and are the more active the more personally vulnerable and fragile I feel . . . God is all the more likely to act through us, the more aware we are of our own helplessness . . . now that the veil of my person is beginning to wear thin (because I feel so vulnerable), I have confidence that God will take over for me somehow (LTF, 104–05).

Like many other mystics Teilhard knew both lassitude and exaltation, agony and ecstasy. Teilhard had discovered a great Other at the center of his being. He knew both the powerlessness of being unable to do anything at all and the ecstasy of being carried along on the great breath that acts *in nobis, sine nobis*—albeit intermittently.

The Cosmic Awakening: La Vision, La Sensation.

Teilhard often referred to the cosmic building process in short cryptic phrases: matter "furls in on itself, interiorizes itself" (HE,96;translation amended); the planet is "coiling up" on itself (P,73); the Universe "folds in on itself" (MPN,32). For Teilhard this building-coiling-folding process takes two forms and both of them are centered about man: "Man *on* whom and *in* whom the universe enfolds itself" (MPN,36). Man is "the two-fold center of the world" (P,31).

The double character of the building process is suggested in the introduction to Teilhard's first essay ("Cosmic Life"). This essay is said to be an effort "to make men *see* and make them *feel (sentir)*." The first section of the essay is titled "The Cosmic Awakening" and it is appropriately divided into sub-sections titled "Vision" *(La Vision)* and "Feeling" *(La Sensation)*.[3]

"Vision" directs our attention to the unities science has shown present in all things. There is the unity of common matter (Teilhard's "reversal" was not yet complete), and this unity was increased with the appearance of life: Life "appeared and develops as a function of the whole universe"; it advances with the "common soul of an evolution." Through this common soul the multiplicity of living forms is further "absorbed in the unity of one and the same general direction" so that all species rise "up a common gradient." This unifying movement is seen to lead to ever more developed nervous systems and on to the formation of the human brain. The brain is seen as center of the cosmic building process. Thus the universe is seen to fold *on* man. This is the vision.

But, Teilhard would urge that it is not enough to observe cosmic currents from the outside, for cosmic currents pervade us and make us what we are. We must come to *feel* them in our own depths. He turns from vision to feeling. Now he allows his consciousness to sweep back within himself "to ascertain whether I might not extend outside myself." He steps into "the deepest recesses of the blackness within" seeking the murmur of the "mysterious waters that rise from the innermost depths." Then with "terror and intoxicating emotion" he realizes that he is not just an observer of cosmic currents, his act of observation is also part of these currents. Influences from all of the earth have poured into his consciousness, affected it, changed it, and will pass on. In passing through they are not out of place, for they make him what he is. He might work to develop himself, but it is a self that has already been developed by the entire history of the earth. His drives, his passions, and his aging proceed by rhythms he cannot control: "My life is not my own." He urges that if we look beneath the superficial way that we ordinarily understand ourselves, we will begin to sense an Unknown One—one hardly emerged from unconsciousness and only half-awake. Seen beneath ourselves in half-shadow the features of this Unknown One seem to merge into the face of the world. Teilhard is stunned by "the vehemence and possessive force of the contact" between his individual self and the universe: gripped "with religious horror" he realizes that "what is emerging in us is the great cosmos" (W,27). This is the Cosmic Awakening: when faced with the *vision* of a unifying cosmos *before* him, he *feels* (or senses) the unifying cosmos *within*. The one who has "once experienced this *vision* can never forget it"; he is like the seaman who has known the intoxicating blue of the South Seas. From now on he longs "for the Absolute whose presence and activity around him he has *felt* for a moment" (W,27; emphasis added).

Thus at the beginning of his first essay Teilhard introduced the duality that runs through all his writings: the "without" that one sees objectively, and the "within" that one feels as his own subjectivity. The cosmos is enfolding *on* man in forming the human brain (the organism, physical and objective); this coiling can be seen from without. The cosmos is enfolding *in* man in forming human consciousness (the awareness, psychic and subjective); this coiling can be felt from within. The objective physical world has developed in the course of evolution—but so has the subject that sees the world. Both are products of evolution. Since subject and object have been developing together in the course of evolution, Teilhard would introduce *The Phenomenon of Man* by saying "the history of the living world can be summarized as the elaboration of ever more perfect eyes (subject) within a cosmos in which there is always something more to be seen (object)" (P,31;parenth. added).

The without and the within are presented under many different names: they are two domains; "external and internal ('objective' and 'subjective') of matter and psyche" (AE,275;F,218), or sometimes matter and spirit, or matter and consciousness. But Teilhard believed many people recognize only one of these domains at the expense of the other. Materialists would acknowledge only the visible world without; they would deny the reality of anything that cannot be seen objectively. On the other hand, "the upholders of a spiritual interpretation" accept only the within, being determined "not to go outside a kind of solitary introspection in which things are only looked upon as being shut in upon themselves in their 'immanent' workings" (P,53). Teilhard would argue that both the without and the within must be recognized; the without because it is evident before us, the within because we are "coincidental with it. We feel it from within . . . It is the thing we know best in the world since we are itself" (HE,93,see also HE,19–20).

The Phenomenon of Man presents a double account of evolution: the development of the without to form the human brain and the development of the within to form human consciousness, and again both developments are central to the universe. *The Phenomenon of Man* begins by telling of the matter in which all things share; such is the "interdependence" among the particles that each "is positively woven from all others" (P,44). Beyond the common matter there are "forces of synthesis" present everywhere so that with the appearance of the first living cells there is a beginning of "a symbiosis or life in common." Through a "network of influences and exchanges" all of the living begin to assume the form of "a sort of diffuse super organism" (P,94). This refers to the interdependence of all the animals and plants that constitute any biome—and to the earth itself as the total biome. Each particular life form has developed only in terms of the whole ecological balance of which it is a part. The totality of inter-related life is called the biosphere. This term is somewhat common. Teilhard extends its meaning in speaking of the biosphere as a single organism:

> Taken in its totality, the living substance spread over the earth
> —from the very first stages of its evolution—traces the lineaments
> of one single and gigantic organism . . . to see life properly we must
> never lose sight of the unity of the biosphere that lies behind the
> plurality and essential rivalry of individual beings. This unity was
> still diffuse in the early stages . . . was to grow ever sharper in
> outline, to fold in upon itself, and, finally, to centre itself under our
> eyes (P,112).

This folding takes place objectively "under our eyes"; it is the vision we see; it has led through developing nervous systems to the formation of the human brain (P,144). The cosmos is folding *on* man (man has emerged "from a general groping of the world . . . from a total effort of life"—P,189).

Just as the total cosmos and its history have developed the present human brain, so the same totality and its history have developed the present human consciousness. The perceptions, hungers, fears, etc., that developed in the course of animal life have become our inheritance. While these have undergone a transformation in becoming reflective and human, they continue to shape our present perceptions (P,179–180). And more significant than this endowment from our genes, our minds have been formed by the entire heritage of thought out of which we have arisen; that is, from the complexity of understandings and values that each has received from his culture and the thought of the earth (P,226). This is "the essence and the totality of a universe deposited within him," within each man (P,180); it is "the inner face of the world" that is "manifest deep within our human consciousness" (P,63).

Since each individual contains the entire history of the earth in his or her physical organism as well as in his or her consciousness, Teilhard would see each individual as a microcosm within the macrocosm. Each person and the earth itself are so intimately bound together that it would be impossible to alter the position of any person (or any other element) within the evolving Whole without rendering that person and the Whole itself "incoherent" (F,61). Each person develops only as part of the developing earth. To even imagine a human consciousness of today present in an earlier geological period would involve one in "a cosmic contradiction" (P,35). The present state of human consciousness requires the present state of the earth to be what it is, and the present earth requires the present consciousness. Teilhard would regard the individual person so intricately involved with the developing world that he would ask if zoologists really discovered the evolution of life in the outside world, "or quite simply and unconsciously have they recognized and expressed themselves in it?" (V,69). But this is true of each of us: "We have found the world in our own souls" (F,17). This is what Teilhard discovered in his inner journey recounted in the previous section: seeking the source of his own power of action he encountered the entire torrent of life that extended far beyond his own individual self.

Since each individual is objectively seen and subjectively felt to be centered, Teilhard would often represent the individual as an ellipse with two foci (figure 3): "a focus of material organization and a focus of psychic centering" (P,61; see also T,167,183,184;AM,241;MPN,121;S,206). The two centers are the two centers around which matter is folding *on* and *in* itself. But just as each person has a *without* and a *within,* so Teilhard would speak of "the *without* and the *within* of the earth" (P,243). The earth also would be presented as an ellipse with its corresponding foci. Each individual is a microcosm and the whole is the macrocosm. Each microcosm finds that "his body" is both his individual body and the whole structured earth; and his soul is both an individual self and the within of the earth that is found in the depths of his consciousness. All four of the foci develop together in function of each other, e.g.: as a person develops the physical earth by one's work, one's individual consciousness becomes more deeply itself. This reciprocity is sometimes suggested in poetic images—as when Matter is imagined as speaking to an individual: "You had need of me in order to grow; and I was waiting for you in order to be made holy" (HU,60). Sometimes it is stated in tortuous prose: "the growth of the *'within'* only takes place thanks to a *double related involution,* the coiling up of the molecule upon itself and the coiling up of the planet upon itself" (P,73).

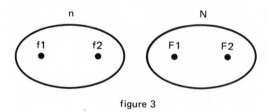

figure 3

The physical structure of the earth is becoming more complex and the psychic structure of the earth is likewise advancing. This psychic structure could be identified as the total context within which the people of today think their individual thoughts; but an individual "cannot think without his or her thought being involved in and combined additively with that of all other thinking beings" (AE,392). In the psyches of individuals a common consciousness is developing, and under the gaze of such individuals a common and increasingly integrated earth is being perceived. So Teilhard will refer to "something greater than ourselves moving forward within us and in our midst." It is the universe folding in and on man. It is a "mega-synthesis" forming "by correlated actions of the *without* and the *within* of the earth" (P,243).

This mega-synthesis can be *seen* objectively without and *felt* subjectively within. This seeing and feeling can sound abstruse till Teilhard speaks of them by more familiar names: *Science* and *Mankind.* Science is the universal objective synthesis seen by the reflective sight developed today; and Mankind is the universal subjective synthesis felt within each separate individual. Science is the common vision that has developed today, it is not the private perspective of any individual or nation; it is a common perspective for humanity. Thus Teilhard would write that the synthesis of science "is fundamentally nothing but a collective act of perception; the world seen in a single coherent perspective by humanity as a whole" (HE,137). It is the universality of the *perspective* that enables those who share this perspective to *feel* in themselves a more universal perceiver: "humanity as a whole," that is, Mankind. Mankind is the "within" of the earth, the within of the macrocosm; it is "the inner face of the world . . . manifest deep within our human consciousness" (P,63). Mankind is "a sort of generalized human personality," (F,32) "an obscure feeling *(sens)* of perpetual growth . . . allied to a need for universal fraternity" (P,245); "a true racial memory, upon which our individual memories draw and through which they complete themselves" (F,32).

Since Science and Mankind are linked as object and subject Teilhard would urge that both came into being together—at the beginning of the last century. Previously there was only a scattering of individuals engaged in scientific research. They were often regarded as eccentrics and their contact with one another was minimal. It was only around eighteen hundred that large numbers of scientists working in different nations became engaged in a common task and developed a common vision that transcended national boundaries. It was precisely in this same period that people began to sense in themselves the reality of something new: Mankind. Before the rise of science it would have taken a prophet to feel *(sentir)* the heartbeat of the embryo of Mankind. But in the nineteenth century Mankind (the *sense* of Man) began to assert itself everywhere. It is present in philosophies such as Comptism and Marxism, and soon revolutions in the name of Mankind began to transform the politics of the globe. Today, more than ever, "terrestrial thought is becoming conscious that it constitutes an organic whole" (T,13). Mankind is already both thinking and acting "through man and above man," so that today "no one can escape being haunted or even dominated" by its presence (AE,38;P, 245). But Teilhard is insistent that this sense of man is linked with the vision of science:

> Taken in the full modern sense of the word, science is the twin sister of mankind. Born together, the two ideas (or the two dreams) grew up together to attain an almost religious valuation in the course of the last century (P,248).

But, just as the two ideas rose together in the previous century, in the present century the two have fallen together into disrepute. They have been judged false gods because of the excesses done in their names. But Teilhard would see that even in disrepute the two ideals continue to support one another; for today whenever people try to justify their hopes for a better world, they instinctively refer to the two-fold dream: Science and Mankind (P,248).

Science and Mankind form a pair for they stand in object-subject relationship: as "man's *vision* is being enlarged" in the Sciences, so "the actual *organ* of this vision" is also perfecting itself (HM,37). Science is the growing unity that the physical world assumes *without,* and Mankind is the corresponding unity that the organ of perception assumes *within.* Teilhard constantly alludes to the pair but does so using many different names: "Science and Humanity," "science and society," (AE,379); "technology and socialization" (M,106;HM,37); "technology and higher co-consciousness" (AE,304). Sometimes he refers to them by phrases: "a single act of vision" and "a single living subject" (F,140); sometimes he hyphenates them into a single word: "technico-social," "technically-socially" (HM,86;AE,327). But in each expression the same two elements are involved: the universal object and the universal subject. And in each case science-technology is mentioned first, for it is the universal object that brings about the universal subject. It is the "coming of science" that is irresistibly "welding people and individuals one to another" (T,20); or "the discoveries of the last hundred years, with their unity of perspective, have brought a new and decisive impetus to . . . our human sense (*notre sens humain)*" (P,267). Thus it is Science that gives rise to Love (the inter-subjective binding power): "impelled by the succession of discoveries . . . our psychology seems to be in course of changing," for we experience "newly freed energies of love" (HE,32). And in order for this universal love to grow and complete Mankind, "it is necessary . . . that we should extend our science to its furthest limits" (P,267).

But just as the new scientific vision gives rise to a new social awareness, it also introduces a new religious awareness. The coming of the Sense of Man is termed "a powerful phenomenon that belongs to the order of religion" (T,23). This new religious development is perhaps the central issue in *The Divine Milieu*. This book on spirituality begins by referring to the recent developments of "the physical sciences" and the consequent sense of human unification: "within us a whole world of affinities and inter-related sympathies . . . is being awakened by the stimulus of these great discoveries." These sympathies are the new Sense of Man, and this "collective awakening . . . must inevitably have a profound religious reaction on the mass of mankind." This profound religious reaction has engendered anxieties in the Christian lest the "human religious ideal" that he finds waking within him should stand in opposition to the "Christian religious ideal" and burst the ancient religion asunder (D,43–46). But this anxiety does not arise because the truths discovered by science might contradict the statements of Christian revelation. Rather, it is that the immensity and unity of what is known is effecting a change *in the knower;* it is awakening within him a common and deeper Self than the self he ordinarily knows.

It is this *sense* of a deeper Self that makes an experience religious; it is what Teilhard means by religion. Thus in "Cosmic Life" the mysterious and unknown Other that he sensed within was sensed "with religious horror." When Teilhard writes of the religion of science, or the mysticism of science (HE,163ff.), or of "mystical treasures hidden in the effort to know" (T,16), or of "worship sustaining the most unbelieving of scientists in his researches" (C,64), he is not implying that what is *known* will be religious, but what is known will give this sense of the mysterious Other as a Knower within the knower. It is the *vision* of a universal and unified Object that enables the seer to *sense* a universal and unified Subject conscious of itself in his or her own human depths. It is the wonders of the objective world that awakens the Other. Science is the first step. This is again why Teilhard would call Science and Religion "two conjugated faces or phases of one and the same complete act of knowledge" (P,285). A complete act of knowledge requires that one first descend into the object known, this descent reverses and gives rise to the *vision* of science; and then one proceeds into the *sense* of the Other whereby the act of knowledge becomes complete. This second phase is religion, mysticism, or adoration.

The first chapter of this study began with a presentation of the Cosmic Sense. This sense reveals "the inner face of the world"; it is "manifest deep within our human consciousness and there reflects upon itself" (P,63). This was said to be the basis for all religion, great poetry, scientific dedication, and prayer. The first man was endowed with this sense and thus could experience an underlying unity as he gazed in wonder at the seas, forests, and stars. Whenever one regards the universe in its entirety, "the mode of its reaction on those who contemplate it is . . . inevitably religious" (C,61). It was an amorphous unity that was seen in former times, so the mode of its reaction was to produce an amorphous pantheism in those who experienced it. But since the time of the first man and woman a vast development has taken place in the way we see. Through science we have acquired a *sense* of spatial immensity, a *sense* of aeons of time, a *sense* of collective unities, etc. (P,33;F,183). All of these senses have been acquired in the recent past and have arisen from the scientific vision of a vast cosmogenesis; the senses named have all come together to form a single sense, the Sense of Man, Mankind. Today we can look at seas, forests, stars, and even oneself through eyes that have been trained to see a common genesis and feel a common destiny. Today the unity of the universe is no longer seen as a formless unity, but as the unity of a single structure. This produces a change within the knower. The Cosmic Sense is still there, but the Cosmic Sense is no longer amorphous. It has become defined like its object to become the Sense of Man. When the universe was seen as an undifferentiated All, the Self that awakened in man as the Cosmic Sense suggested an undifferentiated pantheism. But when the All is known scientifically in its structural unity, the Cosmic Sense becomes structured and is known as the Sense of Man. Thus, the new religion sensed today is the religion of Mankind and it seems to be dominating the world. The "primordial religious energy" associated with pantheism is there, but knowledge has structured it and given it a direction. The religious power of the earth is going through "the crisis of its own discovery" (T,28,24). In the social movements of today it is Mankind that is awakening and calling for worship with all the power of the ancient pantheisms.

This is the mysticism of Science: through experiment with the physical world men and women have been drawn out of themselves and have descended into matter. Through the scientific vision that begins to take shape people feel rising "behind themselves" a new and fascinating seer: Mankind. It is with faith in the future of Man that the people of today are willing to sacrifice themselves. This is the new religion. It is the rising star that is immanent to the earth and it is drawing to itself all of the primordial religious energies of pantheism and threatening to break all other religions asunder. But Teilhard would argue that beyond this sense of the rising All (the Sense of Man) there is a further sense and a further star: the eternal revealing God, the Christic Sense, which is both a "revelation from above" and an "awakening in the heart" (T,23). The "sense of the earth" explodes upward and the "sense of God" takes root downward (F,83). "The sense of man" will react with the "Christic sense" to produce a new Christianity (T,33).

Three Reflections

Teilhard tells of standing in the mist of a September evening in 1917 watching the distant line of war. He had already been in the trenches many times and there, facing danger, he experienced the drunken exhilaration of a great freedom. Now as he watched distant trails of rising smoke he experienced nostalgia for the Front; he was attracted again by the "fascinating and deadly line," the "sacred line of banked-up earth," and he tried to understand why. At the Front there was a common and all-engaging task; thus he was freed from his individual concerns and the burden of social conventions. But the freedom did not end there for he sensed an "immense human Presence," "a Soul greater than his own," Mankind, "born above all in hours of crisis." Teilhard would argue that as soon as someone:

> takes up his place on the sacred circumference of the truly active World, a personality of another order is disclosed, which masks and effaces the everyday man. The man of the Front acts as a function of the whole Nation and of all that lies hidden behind the Nations . . . Such a man has concrete evidence to prove that he no longer lives for himself—that he is freed from himself—that another Thing lives in him and dominates him. I do not hesitate to say that this special disindividuation which enables the fighting man to attain some human essence higher than himself is the ultimate secret of the incomparable feeling of freedom that he experiences and that he will never forget (HM,176).

The reference to a "sacred circumference" picks up the image of the circle from the last chapter. It is to the front line of war that one makes the descent and there accordingly one finds what is always found at the base of the descent: risk, passion, nourishment and energy. Each of these is found at the Front (W,174–75;J,223). But beyond these, and in a reverse direction, Teilhard sensed Humanity being born; it seemed as though a window opened on what Man is becoming: "a higher Thing of great nobility" that is still in process of formation. But an ambiguity remained in Teilhard's wartime thought: is Humanity a "Thing" or is it a "Soul" ("a personality of another order")? Years later Teilhard would judge Humanity itself to be more or less a thing, a collectivity. But to this collectivity Christ would give his Soul. Thus Teilhard would frequently argue for the reality of the human collectivity and then call for something further: Unanimity—and the root meaning of the term is having a *single* soul (AE,72,372;P,251;V,266;AM,256ff.). Thus there are three steps in an ever more interior sequence: first, there is "the everyday man"; then, "a higher Thing" (Humanity as collectivity), and, finally, "a Soul greater than my own" (Christ as Unanimity). Teilhard would present these as "three successive zones of increasing interiorization," or "three successive phases" of reflection: First, there is "The human (or the reflective)": then, there is "The Ultrahuman (or the co-reflective)": then, there is "The Christic (or the pan-reflective)" (AE,375ff). These phases are often implicit in the writings of Teilhard (see T,213–14;HE,72–84), and are a continuous theme in the final years of his unpublished Journals where they are abbreviated as R1,R2 and R3. R1 is the single reflecting individual; R2 is Humanity, the collectivity that shares a common vision; R3 is Christ, the Soul of souls—also identified as Revelation.[4] R2 and R3 are "higher" or "deeper" selves than one's "everyday" self, so they are felt religiously. This gave rise to the conflict presented in *The Divine Milieu* (and treated in the previous section) wherein R2, the "human religious ideal" and R3, the "Christian religious ideal" were dividing people's faith. The conflict is resolved by placing the two as successive phases in an ever more interior sequence.

In the sequence from R1 to R2 the individual first comes out of himself, only to sense Mankind and thereby to have entered more deeply into himself. We cannot become completely reflective except by being reflected in one another (F,202,see P,263). Only through others "can one discover his own depths. Reflection . . . is essentially a social phenomenon" (F,138). It is when we set ourselves up as autonomous Titans (R1) that we allow our true selves (R2,R3) to go unrealized. The movement from R2 to R3 proceeds in the same inward direction: the individual "implodes upon itself" and passing through the collective attains its paroxysm in "a mysterious super-ego" (HM,38); "within its own infinitesimal ego . . . accession to the Christic Ego" (HM,95). "At the center of my own small *ego*" there is the irresistible rise "of a sort of Other who would be even more I than I am myself" (HM,82,transl. amended). This Other is God experienced as a *plus moi même,*"—"a greater myself" (D,89). Humanity has revealed itself in each person's own depths, now God as Other reveals Himself in the depths of Humanity. The sequence has taken place "within." Our consciousness itself has grown bright with God, now we "worship in ourselves something that is 'us,' God with us" (W,187). By the Incarnation the transcendent God does not attach himself externally to the universe, rather, he appears where the universe is most "inward"—in Mankind. And there he is not present as an "outside supplement," but comes through an "internal metamorphosis" of the human substance (W,188). "Does the Master break down doors to enter his own home?" No, when the divine Flame appears to light up our world, it lights it from within (HU,23). God is not added extrinsically to the developing world: he is sensed as "rising" or "emerging" from the depths. He seems to be born in the Heart of Matter—rather—he is born *as* the Heart of Matter.

With the appearance of the reflective individual (R1), the earth is said to have found its soul (P,183). But it does not attain its "Soul of souls," its "higher soul," its "unanimity," until R3. R3 is "a soul that superanimates all the assembled souls" (HM,78). That is, R3 super-animates R2 (the assembled R1's). *In itself,* Humanity is without a soul.[5] This is why the ideal of Humanity can appear cold and impersonal; it is only a collectivity until Christ gives it the warmth of a Heart. Thus Teilhard carried with him a picture of the Sacred Heart: it was on his work table when he died. It showed "Christ offering his heart to men" (see HU,42), or in the shorthand of Teilhard, Christ is offering R3 to R2. It is only because of that Heart at the goal of evolution that the whole becomes a process that one can love.

The sequence of the reflections could be misleading, for there are significant ways R3 would come before R2: In Teilhard's own life he tells of knowing the revealed Christ long before he knew Humanity (HM,15,

31); likewise, *The Divine Milieu* first considers "a soul envisaged as alone in the world before God" (D, 140), (R1 alone before R3) and onlythen does it consider the soul's relations with other men (R1's relations with R2). In history Christ was revealed in the first century while Humanity did not appear until the nineteenth. The underlying truth is that the revealing God (R3) was present from the first moment of creation. But in the order of phenomenon or vision, R3 *appears* only late in the process after R2 even though it had been active all along:

> When Christ appears in the clouds he will simply be manifesting a metamorphosis that has been slowly accomplished under his influence in the heart of the mass of mankind (D, 128).

The sequence of R1, then R2, then R3 might lead one to the idea that God (R3) became a reality only late in the evolutionary process. This idea has characterized some forms of process theology so that other writers have envisioned God coming into being only through the process. Teilhard prays:

> Lord, in your mercy you gave me to see that this idea is false, and that I must overthrow it if I were ever to have sight of you . . . In the beginning was the *Word*, supremely capable of mastering and moulding whatever might come into being in the world of matter . . . So, far from light emerging gradually out of the womb of our darkness, it is the Light, existing before all else was made which, patiently, surely, eliminates our darkness (HU, 21).

Teilhard emphasizes the point by saying, "This is the truth." The revealing Word has been drawing matter into form since the beginning, and the whole groping movement of life is matter's response to what has been revealed to it. The final stage of interiority was there from the beginning, but appearance shows matter furling in on itself in an inward flux producing ever new degrees of interiority as it advances. But "this flux is a tide produced by the action of a supreme star. If the multiple is unified, it is ultimately because it is *subject to a pull*" (AE, 146).

The pull that has been acting on all matter and drawing it together in center-to-center contact is identified as the attraction of love. In the beginning this love could hardly be distinguished from molecular forces.

But even among the molecules, love was the building power that worked against entropy, and under its attraction the elements groped their way towards union. Thus, "the most telling and profound way of describing the history of the universe would undoubtedly be to trace the evolution of love" (HE,33). Other forms of union are external and do not advance the process of interiorization. "Love alone is capable of uniting living beings in such a way as to complete and fulfill them, for it takes them and joins them by what is deepest in themselves" (P,265). Now it is humans who are groping towards one another and under the attraction of love they often grope blindly and do not succeed. Instinctively, they try again, for the command given to all the elements in the beginning was "Love one another." And from the union that would be formed the loving elements have always expected to give rise to something greater than themselves. Thus, the command to love both God and our fellow man is not a command superimposed by the Gospel upon the movement of life. Rather the command tells of "Life itself, life in the integrity of its aspirations" (F,82). Teilhard would apply the phrase of Christ, "I did not come to abolish but to fulfill," to Christ as fulfilling the whole development of the cosmos. The religion of a united mankind rising from the earth and joining people together in love is also the religion of the transcendent God. "No man can love his neighbor without drawing nearer to God." "It is impossible to love Christ without loving others," and it is impossible "to love others . . . without moving nearer to Christ" (F,98;D,144). Thus through R2 one moves nearer to R3, and only in R3 can mankind achieve its unanimity.

In the love between a man and a woman the two find they are no longer "reflective monads": they form an "affective dyad" (See HM,60;T,70). However, in forming a dyad or pair they are still incomplete, but their completion will not be extrinsic to their union: "without coming out of itself, the pair will find its equilibrium only in a third being ahead of it," that is, in God. God is the consolidation of their love and the deeper soul wherein the two souls are united: "Love is a three term function: man, woman and God" (HE,76).

Since R2 precedes R3 Teilhard would not allow that religion is a purely individual matter; religion is essentially social. "We are united to Christ by entering into communion with all men" (S,77). Teilhard became a Christian through a close communion with another; it was through his mother that Christianity came to inflame his soul as a child (HM,41).

Religious traditions always contain more than a common perspective, they contain *"experiences of contact* with a supreme Inexpressible which they preserve and pass on" (AE,242). If these traditions shared only a common teaching they would form only a collectivity, but beyond this there is an experience of contact which resides in the religious community. In any community with a touch of common soul (e.g., the two lovers above) there is a bit of the revelation of God.

Thus revelation involves a direct contact with God, but not a contact "confined to the individual, but one as . . . all-embracing as the whole human entity" (T,36). Teilhard alludes to the familiar phrase, "Religion is a strictly personal matter," where personal means private or individual. He rejects this "individualist stance" and even goes so far as to suggest that the solitary individual is an agnostic (C,118;V,140,142). Religion is not for the solitary Titan, it "is related to and coextensive with not the individual man, but the whole of mankind." For religion "there cannot be any subject other than the totality of thought on earth" (C,119;see H,47):

> I would not be so foolish as to seek to build up science by my own unaided efforts. Similarly, my own effort to reach faith can succeed only when contained within a total human experience and prolonged by it (C,119).

Religion must finally be the act of R2,Humanity itself. "Religion ought to be phyletic" (J,15/Sept/52). Both the individual and the limited group are too confined for what is truly religious. Some form of religion is involved whenever the solitary Titan moves away from his isolation to become part of a wider subject; this wider subject might be a loving dyad, it might be Humanity and so forth. But religion is complete only when the wider subject is the transcendent God radiating at the heart of Humanity.

Throughout the evolutionary process matter has been furling in on itself, interiorizing itself. And ultimately, there will be "the wholesale internal introversion upon itself of the Noosphere" (P,287). Evolution is the process in which matter, the "without," becomes interiorized as the "within." The sequence begins with matter, proceeds to consciousness, to reflective consciousness, to co-consciousness, and finally to Omega, the "universal focus . . . of psychic interiorization" (MPN,116). Since matter is interiorizing itself into psyche, evolution might be described as a movement from Matter as ultimate known Object into Christ as ultimate knowing Subject. Thus evolution is a vast act of knowing in which the universe is first gathered into the synthesizing gaze of humanity, and humanity is gathered into the synthesizing gaze of Christ. "I cannot define the world for myself other than as a gradual awakening of consciousness" (UP,LaMare,25/Apr/31). "A consciousness gradually waking by way of countless fumblings, this would, in this case, be the essential picture of evolution" (V,181).[6]

Matter is groping its way to interiorization. In coming to reflection in man (R1) the world finds its soul; in forming Mankind the world becomes co-reflective (R2); finally it implodes on the "universal focus . . . of psychic interiorization" (MPN,116). Christ is thus the final within, the ultimate Subject, to which all things have been moving. Christ is the one all mystics have felt as the "center of complete reflection coinciding with what mysticism has since all time called the revelation of God" (AE,296).[7]

Though the movement from the individual to God is a movement of increasing interiorization, the "without" has an essential part to play in it all. Each individual begins with his or her own small focus of consciousness. Leaving this focus, each person must proceed *out* of himself into the immensity and dangers of the universe, onto "the sacred circumference." Veils of conventional answers are removed so that one sees into Matter; to the radical "without" in its frightening energy. Soon the individual realizes that a larger focus than its own individual ego is necessary to contain it all ("it required a spirit more perfect than mine to dominate and comprehend"). When an individual is on the sacred circumference he feels a deeper subject awakening within. It is Humanity divided and troubled, dominating and comprehending the cosmos. But deeper than the heartless groping of Humanity it is also God revealing himself as the Universal Heart of Matter and tenderly drawing all things into himself. This is the Christ, the conscious focus of the Noosphere. The process began in the individual's psychic center (R1) and proceeds into the 'without' of the cosmos. Then it reverses and rises into the psychic Center of the cosmos. The process is familiar. It is the cycle of descent and reascent. One descends to the circumference in order to rise within to the God who fills all things. This is the basic movement by which one achieves salvation through matter: through entering matter at its lowest untrodden depths (apart from the overlays of conventional form) one reverses and implodes within to the Heart of all things. In more familiar terms: what is being described is an act of perception. This act happens across human consciousness or as human consciousness, but Christ is the great Perceiver.

Perception Becomes Reflection

During the course of this study Teilhard has been shown to contrast three sets of opposing positions: Chapter Two spoke of two types of knowers: one type knows by abstract and timeless principles, while the other knows by a perception of the physical and temporal world. Then, Chapter Three presented two types of people: the juridicist who appeals to personal values derived from an extrinsic revelation, and the pantheist who appeals to the tangible evidence of the impersonal All. The present chapter has told of the opposition between those who acknowledge the spiritual, but limit themselves to a solitary introspection of the "within," and the materialists who recognize only the external appearance of the "without."

The three sets of oppositions are not identical, but the different groups can be combined so that on the one hand there are those whose knowledge concerns the abstract, the juridical, the "within;" and on the other there are those whose knowledge concerns the real, the physical, the "without." Those who limit themselves to the first way of knowing have one thing in common: they refuse to acknowledge matter; they refuse to take seriously their experience of the objective physical world. Those who limit themselves to the second way of knowing refuse to acknowledge the reality of their own human consciousness; they do not see that any understanding of the physical world must also include an understanding of their own psyche. For Teilhard, each group would confine itself to one half of the problem. For those in the first group objective experience is discredited so that all truth becomes like the truths of geometry: it is all based on "postulates"—more or less arbitrary assumptions. These assumptions can be said to be a matter of revelation (accepted on "blind faith"), or of personal preference ("Religion is a strictly personal matter"), or on the general assent of some group ("common opinion"). The moral systems of those in the first group are likewise free of any objective evidence; it is all a matter of "divine commandment," or "personal option," or "social convention." Since there are many people who think this way, there have arisen many conflicting geometries, many conflicting theologies, and many conflicting moralities. Each of them appears equally valid for each is equally free of evidence. Those who think this way could be said to be imprisoned in their own *cogito*—or in the common *cogito*s of the group to which they belong; (*cogito* and related Latin words are not used by Teilhard, they are introduced here to explicate his thought—see, however, J,4/Mar/51). The geometries, theologies, and moralities of such people would be their *cogitata*. These people live within the systems they have either "received" or invented, but apart from these systems, they are agnostic. They have restricted their thinking to a personal-spiritual world, only to find that without matter they "waste away in the outlook to which they confine themselves; they die of inanition" (HU,61). If they are Christians, they find that even their Christianity hides the world from their sight (Lf,25). Perhaps they find great comfort in their faith, but they have not explored its truth. They have allowed "a veil of conventional answers to cover the mysteries of life . . . to avoid the anxiety that contact with reality might renew in them" (HE,19).

The only way that a Christian—or a "believer" of any sort—may avoid living in such a world is by opening his or her eyes to see beyond the veil of convention and contact the untrodden earth. The individual must come out of him or herself and out of the "human" universe to experience "the" universe. The person's "within" must descend to the "without" and experience "Reality entire and untamed" by human answers. The individual must be an explorer—one who comes to know that human answers and conventional structures are not enough. Thereby the person makes a descent from the *cogitata* into the *percepta*. The Christian believer is particularly alarmed, for in descending "into the great ocean of Matter, (he) is afraid that he may see his God burst asunder" (HM,56). In descending into matter one must proceed "away from divine realities."

We often prefer to remain in the personal intimacy of our *cogito,* for descending into the *percepta* will involve us in anxieties without end. But, if we are to respond to the call of matter, "we must *plunge boldly* into the vast current of things" (W,28). In making the plunge we seem to have lost our very selves in the vast impersonality of matter; "through the staggering vastness of its dimensions" we receive "the first and most violent shock that tends to overwhelm us" (AE,185). Our thought tries to conceive of a space that is measured in millions of light years and becomes "engulfed in the enormous anonymity of the stellar bodies" (AM,268). Or we turn our attention to the infinitesimal intricacies of the atoms and find that their number and movements defy all human conception. These two infinities (suspected in the seventeenth century) filled the soul of Pascal with existential dread. But the science of our own day has revealed the immense abysses of geological time and unnumbered billions of living creatures extending over billions of years; modern science has discovered infinities that Pascal never suspected. In these staggering dimensions the personal world of the *cogito* seems to have dissolved into nothingness. Our original fears of the experience of matter seem to have been justified. Man, having entered the world of science and experiment seems "definitely to redissolve in the common ground of things" (AM,268):

> Which of us has ever in his life really had the courage to look squarely at and try to 'live' a universe formed of galaxies whose distance apart runs into hundreds of thousands of light years? Which of us, having tried, has not emerged from the ordeal shaken in one or other of his beliefs . . . has not had a confused sensation of a gigantic shadow passing over the serenity of his joy? (P,227).

To "live" this universe one must "renounce the comfort of familiar narrowness" and know the feeling "of being crushed by the enormities of the cosmos" (P,226–27). In confronting the physical world one "never knows what power he is unleashing"; matter is "the fire that consumes and the water that overthrows." We seem either lost in a chaos without order or caught in the heartless determinism of a cosmic machine:

> We are terrified, too, when we see that mechanization may bring an end that is as much to be dreaded as a death through disintegration and return to 'Prime Matter' . . . we feel that we are caught up in the gyrations of some infernal circle (HM,50).

In living these fears Man has finally emerged from the imaginings of his *cogito* and the juridical world of his own *cogitata*. He has come out of the personal or the inter-personal world formed by human subjectivities and entered the impersonal vastness of the All. In a confused and troubled state he has descended into the depths of matter. He can never again know untroubled worship or the religion that is a "private matter." But not knowing these—he might know God! In coming into the universe Man has been thrown into dimensions beyond his ability to imagine—and that is his salvation. He has come into the staggering world of matter and will never be the same; he is no longer a juridicist or theologian, even all personal privacy is gone. Matter has changed him and opened him; matter "by overflowing and dissolving our narrow standards of measurement reveal(s) to us the dimensions of God" (HU,69). It is the "physicists" who are the mystics; it is only through contact with the physical world that one can ever become a true mystic.

Experimental science has drawn man out of his personal world, and in the process seems to have dissolved his own importance in the infinity of impersonal matter. But contact with the immensity of matter and geological time has gradually led experimental scientists to become aware of another immensity: the immense movement of ascending life. Matter itself is seen to have undergone a vast transformation throughout the geological ages; there is evidence of "a universal and stubborn movement depicted in the successive layers of dead matter and the present spread of the living." And man, who had seemingly dissolved forever into the crucible of universal matter, "is in process of re-emerging from his return into the crucible, more than ever *at the head of nature*" (AM,268). Now the other star, the one that the materialists could not accept, reveals itself in power. With "religious horror" the "physicist" senses a vast Subject drawing the terrifying immensities of the cosmos into its own infinite Center. The ardent Center of the macrocosm is *felt* as the Center of the microcosm. The "physicist" trembles to sense at the depths of his consciousness "Christ . . . radiating *physically* over the terrifying totality of things" (see HM,94).[8]

Teilhard has asked which of us has tried to live a universe formed of uncounted galaxies? Those who might have tried know that no human fragment is able to live such a universe, either personally or collectively. But a mysterious Other sensed at the depths of Mankind lives that universe. This Other knows that universe and knows that he knows: this is the Third Reflection, the Christ. The individual has become suddenly aware that the terrifying immensities of matter are throbbing with a single life, as though "a sort of bloodstream or nervous system" ran through it all. "The entire universe (is) vibrant" (HU,43). One has discovered Cosmic Life—and it is personal! The risen Christ is pulsating through all things and is drawing them into his own exuberant unity. The individual trembles with "the inner terrors of a metamorphosis." The individual has lost himself in the objective immensities of matter only to find that through his Humanity these very immensities are being drawn into an immense Someone. The immense terror awakened by the descent into matter is transformed into the immensity of a single desire. The *cogito* cannot deal with a passion of such magnitude. Filled with that which it cannot grasp, contain or imagine, the *cogito* cries out with the voice of all creation and "with a desire as vast as the universe: 'In truth, you are my Lord and my God' " (HU,34). Aware that a loving Person is the Center of all things, the individual no longer fears the dimensions of the cosmos, they have become the dimensions of his prayer:

> Greater still, Lord, let your universe be greater still, so that I may hold you and be held by you in a contact at once made ever more intense and ever wider in extent! (D,47).

Teilhard would commit himself *to the world;* for it is through "discovering, fashioning, and experiencing the world" as object that one is able "to penetrate ever further" into Christ the knowing Subject (HU,36). Science in itself does not discover Christ, but only Christ can satisfy the yearnings born in the hearts of those formed in the school of science. (S,36).

One enters the world of matter only with a perception that takes one beyond all "conventional answers." Each individual can have such an experience. Perhaps it is a moment of great distress that lets an individual know his or her own conventional answers are not enough; each must then grope to a new awareness. The scientist in his research knows the power of the conventional answer; and finds in himself the tendency to find only what he is expected to find. But, perhaps one day the scientist will stand alone before a single fact that no one has seen before, and that science cannot explain. He will be disoriented by his discovery, but at that moment of disorientation he might sense a mighty Someone waking in his depths and calling him to form a wider comprehension of the universe. The moment is religious. Science is the way of descent into the cosmic Object, it faces out; religion is the way of ascent into the cosmic Subject, it faces in. Together they form "the two conjugated faces or phases of one and the same complete act of knowledge" (P,285).

The previous chapter told of two stars whose meanings developed in various ways, but whose basic identification was that of *All* and *Person.* Now the two stars can be further identified: the All is the Object of all knowledge, the *Percepta;* and the Person is Christ, the Subject of all knowing, the *Perceptor.* The previous chapter then set elements from the writings of Teilhard into three parallel columns:

All	*Becoming*	*Person*
Earth	Humanity	God
Past	Present	Future

But the identification of these columns was not complete. Perhaps the real significance of all these triads is found in the following additions.

Percepta	*Percipiens*	*Perceptor*
Cosmos as *Object* (seen)	Humanity perceiving	Christ as *Subject* (sensed)

One begins the process when conventional answers seem irrelevant and one goes apart from humanity's caravan routes to face the universe alone. That is, one is drawn out of the reflexive *cogito* to descend into the *Percepta*. Only now—out of oneself (drawn "from his own center to center him on the universe" HE, 168)—is one truly able to come together with others who have made the same descent. These rise together to constitute "humanity grouped by the act of discovery"; these are the *Percipiens*. The "speculative" individual who remains apart from all experience accepts or rejects God as a matter of blind faith—or remains agnostic. But when the individual leaves such speculation and blindness and descends to matter he will rise together with others in a common human awareness. Together they will sense the great *Perceptor*, as it were, "behind" themselves (W, 182). It is only by finally *seeing* the *Percepta* that Humanity is formed, and it will be this unified Humanity that will *sense* the Christ—the great *Perceptor* in its common human depths.

The previous chapter argued that the movement of evolution can be summarized by reading the three columns across: thus, *All* is *Becoming* a *Person,* or *Matter* rises as *Spirit* to *God,* and so forth. But Teilhard also urged that evolution can be understood as a vast psychic exercise (HE, 23). This psychic exercise is now seen to be a divine act of perception. Again one could read the columns across: the *Percepta* is rising through Humanity's act of *perceiving* into the divine *Perceptor*. Matter strives to be perceived (become Thought) so that it might enter the great Thinker. The long history of the galaxies, the whole evolution of life, the rise of the mammals, and our own human gestures of research are thus phases in a vast act of divine perception. In this act, Christ is the great Perceiver —but what he perceives is not yet clear. And, in the process, if humans are only making gestures, is it evolution, the universe, or God who is finally the one acting?

When Teilhard wrote of the two stars (first and third column) he also claimed they would come into conjunction. Such a conjunction would necessitate that the *Percepta* coincide with the *Perceptor!* This conjunction would mean that the divine-cosmic act of perception (that has just been identified) is really a divine-cosmic act of *reflection:* that is, *God perceiving himself reflected in matter.* Thus, matter is not the final object seen—it could not be, for matter has no being in itself. Matter is only the reflector of Being; it "reverses" the light; it is the mirror in which the great Subject knows himself. This is the Third Reflection: God knows himself as reflected on matter. At the present time this reflection is incomplete as the mirror is in fragments. Only through the growing unification of Humanity can the mirror be restored; this is the second reflection ("The Second Reflection: . . . the mirror that enables to better see God" J, 12/Nov/50).

When the Second Reflection was developed in this study, Science was identified as the universal *object* known and Mankind as the universal *subject* knowing. With this understanding Teilhard had seen great significance in the International Geophysical Year: he called it "a pan-Human gesture in its subject, Humanity, and in its object, the Planet" (J, 12/Dec/54). But when it is stated in this way the *reflective* nature of the act is not evident. Scientific knowing manifests its reflective character through the reversal that Teilhard sees presently taking place in contemporary physics, biology and sociology. In these fields science is discovering that the whole Subject-Object dichotomy ("Man on one side, the world on the other") is no longer valid. Now by "doubling back and reflection, the subject of yesterday is about to become the principle object of tomorrow" (HE, 114–15; translation amended). In seeing evolution, consciousness is seeing its own identity; scientists are suspecting that the structure they perceive is "the reflection of their own thought" (P, 32). They are not finding matter itself but the thought forms they were imposing on matter (see Chapter Two). Matter is only a mirror:

> The stuff of the universe examined as a close texture, resolved itself into a mist in which reason could no longer grasp, in what remained of the phenomena, anything but the forms that it had itself imposed

on them. In the final issue, mind found itself once again face to face
with its own reflection (HE,174).

When this discovery is complete it will constitute the Second Reflection:
Humanity will know Humanity. Mind will know its own reflection. This
"reversal" will involve a complete change in the fundamental way men
have values and act. This reflection will involve "inner tortures"; for "the
earth will only become conscious of itself through the crisis of conversion"
(HE,38).

The Third Reflection cannot be stated with the same simplicity as the
second because the subject and the object of this reflection are not entirely
identical—yet they must be identical in some sense or the act would not
be reflection at all. In the Third Reflection the object known will be *God*
("God will become the true object of science" J,8/Mar/51); but the subject
knowing will be *Christ,* the God-Man. The act is reflection because God as
subject will know God as object; but in Christ man has been introduced as
co-subject in God's knowing of himself. "In heaven we ourselves shall
contemplate God, but, as it were, through the eyes of Christ" (D,114).
"The beatific vision will be . . . the Divine revealing itself to each one of
us through the eyes of Christ" (S,77; see also C,67). Thus the final *Percepta*
will be God, but the final *Perceptor* will be Christ, the God-Man. The
universe has been created so that the great Perceptor might be formed;
God has from the beginning been "preparing for himself the faculty
destined to perceive Him," that is, the eyes of Christ (J,204). This cosmic
reflective process could be presented in an image: light would radiate out
from God into the depths of matter; then it would be reflected back (the
"reversal") and rise into the eyes of Christ. Thus Teilhard writes of the
great Center: everything "descends from it as from a peak of transcendence," and to it "everything climbs as to a focus of immanence" (HE,70).
The transcendence would be God and the immanence would be the eyes of
Christ. Thus, Omega, the final term of the Universe, is both immanent
and transcendent (see P,271). Teilhard would call it "the mysterious
double point," "the double heart of the world" (HM,49;J,24/Oct/
51;28/Oct/51).

God's descent into the lowest part of the earth and subsequent return
has been called the "divine cycle"; now it is seen as the Third Reflection.
The "natural cycle" by which Humanity will know Humanity is said to

resemble the divine cycle. And it is only through the natural cycle that the divine cycle is complete: "God folds back on the creature at the same time as the creature folds back on itself" (UP, E. LeRoy, Aug. 1929); In his Journal Teilhard writes of the "Circuit ΩK" (he has drawn an ellipse around his symbols for Omega and the Cosmos). This circuit refers to the divine act of reflection; the circuit gives a curious cyclic flavor to the thought of Teilhard—all is involved in a vast descent and return. Thus, *The Phenomenon of Man* sees the elements of the world achieving a "*re*union" for they are in an "evolutionary cycle" (P, 253). All things are seen to "*re*ascend the slope of Being." Consciousness will "*re*-emerge," there will be a "*re*storation," a "*re*collection," a "*re*turn" (W, 41, 52, 81). Thus, things are "rising again," being brought back or taken back (D, 86, 104, 119), being "reunited" (D, 115, 122).

Since this rising again constitutes human perception, Teilhard would seem to be writing with a similar understanding to that found in the poem in the Introduction of this study. The poem tells Everyman:

> And thus in thee the circuit vast
> Is rounded and complete at last.

But for Teilhard the circuit will be rounded and complete only when the circle of Humanity is rounded and complete.[9]

When the mystic looks at the present universe he or she sees God reflected everywhere for "nature is a thousand reflections of God" (J, 206). But many mystics do not recognize it is only a reflection; in pursuing only matter they "turn their backs on the rising sun" (HE, 174); they pursue only "the reflection of the sun" (C, 124). Those who pursue a woman only for the pleasure in her body "are deceived by a reflection" (HU, 70). All of these will come to discover that they have been reduced to dust and dust is all they hold. They have not realized that the two stars must come together; that is, they have not realized that their act of perception is ultimately an act of reflection. When Teilhard found the universe to be only a reflector, the stars came together in an explosion of dazzling flashes. Since the universe is a "mirror" Teilhard would claim that the universe is God for him or the universe is dust for him depending only *on how the divine ray falls;* by his reversal he knew "the only reality which can satisfy us lies beyond the transparencies in which it is mirrored" (D, 120).

The divine radiance shimmers over the surface of matter; it is perceived and begins to rise as human science; then, beyond this phase it must continue to rise as human religion. The vast phenomenon of religion is only "the long disclosure of God's Being through the collective experience of the whole of humanity" (HE,47). God is felt in human depths "reflecting himself personally"; God is seeing Himself with human vision and thus with the eyes of Christ.

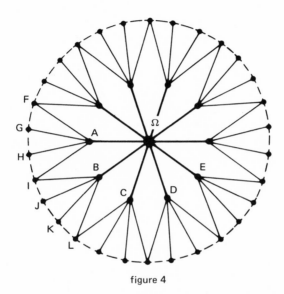

figure 4

Teilhard often uses the image of a circle or of a sphere to represent the universe: one must descend to "the sacred circumference" in order to rise to the Center; one must *see* the vastness of its inner surface in order to *feel* the central focus; one must universalize in order to rise along the radii to the personal Center, and so forth. These understandings could be diagrammed in conjunction with figure 4, first presented in Chapter One. Omega is the central Soul of souls; and A,B,C,D, etc. are the assembled individual souls (the mystical Body); F,G H,I, etc. are the elements of matter (the cosmic Body). The process of knowing begins when an individual, A, looks at the inner surface. The individual is drawn by what he or she sees and so descends to F,G,H,I, ("when the world reveals itself to us it draws us to itself"), only to find that he or she holds nothing but dust (F,G,H,I). At the moment of *seeing* the nothingness of matter one *senses* the great All is really behind one at Omega ("immediately behind us, as though it were an extension of ourselves" W,182). This is the moment of which innumerable mystics have spoken, the moment of *todo y nada,* the moment when the dust of Nothingness ("the stuff of the universe resolves itself into a mist") is replaced by infinite Being. For Teilhard it is the moment of reversal, the moment when the nothingness of the Object—of all objects—is apparent and the infinite Being of the divine Subject asserts itself "behind us." After the reversal one advances inward by the synthetic power of the human gaze ("the dust cloud of experience . . . is kindled at the fire of knowledge"). Those who have descended to "the sacred circumference" *feel* themselves drawing together with other explorers ("humanity grouped by the act of discovery"). These are assembled at their depths to form a circle of centers (A,B,C,D, etc., a circle of "peaks of the spirit"). Christ radiates at the Center as "Soul of souls": the collectivity is given unanimity.

Just as the synthetic power of the human gaze draws the dust of the universe together, so the synthetic power of Christ's gaze draws the dust of mankind together. As his eyes fall over the circle of Mankind he becomes the "Savior of human unity":

> Christ consumes with his glance my entire being. And with that same glance . . . those who are around me and whom I love. Thanks to him therefore I am united with them . . . through their inmost selves . . . Christ *binds* us and *reveals* us to one another (W,110–11).

Christ's gaze is the binding power, the "reverse gravity" that gives consistency to human dust. As humanity has imposed form on matter by its perception, so Christ by his perception has imposed his form on us ("the dust cloud of experience takes form"). The *Forma Christi* is imposed and Mankind-Spirit is the "true matter" that receives it. In the depths of Humanity "God (is) bent over the now intelligent mirror of earth to impose on it the first marks of his beauty" (HE,47).

Teilhard has written an imaginative account of a time of prayer before a picture of Christ that is hanging on the wall of a church. As he prays he begins to see an aureole of radiance spread from the image of Christ "to the outermost spheres of the realm of matter" (HU,43). Gradually, Teilhard becomes aware that "the center of the radiance and irridescence was hidden in the transfigured portrait's eyes." Over the eyes in rainbow hues passes the reflection or Idea of everything that has power to charm men. The radiation begins to reverse. Then the eyes begin to gather in "all the glances that have warmed and mirrored back a human heart." They become so gentle that it seems to him that his mother is standing before him; they change to become the passionate and pure eyes of a woman; they change again to become the noble and virile eyes of a man of great courage, refinement and strength. The eyes of all humanity are being gathered to form the eyes of Christ. But soon Teilhard is dumbfounded: "Little by little an extraordinary expression, of great intensity, spread over the diverse shades of meaning which the divine eyes revealed." This new expression draws all other eyes into itself. The final expression is indecipherable: it tells of either "an indescribable agony or of a superabundance of triumphant joy." Teilhard would later see the same expression in the eyes of a dying soldier. But the vision has ended and the picture on the church wall has regained its familiar outline.

The final stage of the ascent to the Center occurs only with human death; an indecipherable moment of "indescribable agony" or of "triumphant joy." In death one makes a final descent into the depths of matter. But the person of faith believes that it does not end there. The great paradox of matter makes its final reflection—death is transformed into life—and one rises into the eyes of Christ.

Chapter Five

COMMUNION
The Sequence of Growth and Diminishment

During his wartime service Teilhard was part of the "huge masses of mankind that were then facing one another in the trenches of France, from the Yser to Verdun" (HM,31). But beneath the conflicts of war Teilhard sensed a rise of love-energy forming the unity of man. All of the elements of war, the banked-up earth of the trenches, the aircraft flying through exploding shrapnel, and the distant tables of diplomats, were seen as part of a cosmic process, the "noble and silent transformation of Nature" (MM,110). Teilhard had long studied the history of Nature's transformation in the layers of rock. He had become aware of an age-old movement between Life and Death and through it all the earth making a stubborn rise to spirit. Now, in the trenches of war, he judged himself privileged to share in the deeds wherein the cosmic process was reaching its completion. He was in communion with both an enormous growth and an awesome diminishment: Nature was refining its essence.

Growth: the Radial Function of the Tangential
Teilhard divides energy into two basic types: the first would be the energy known by the physicists; this is the energy of the "without" that Teilhard would call tangential energy. The tangential energy present in a system is a measure of its structure. Tangential energy "links the element with all others of the same order (that is to say, of the same complexity and the same centricity) as itself in the universe" (P,65; parenthesis in text). This energy is subject to entropy for structures break down, disorder increases, and energy dissipates in disorder. The second energy is the spiritual

energy of consciousness; it is the energy of the "within." Teilhard would call it axial or radial energy.

Radial energy works in opposition to the movement of entropy; it gathers diverse elements together and binds them into ever more comprehensive unities. Radial energy is the "arranging form of energy (energy of invention and combination" V,254). It is the energy of evolution; it is the "physico-moral energy of personalization" (HE,72); the love energy presented in the previous chapters. It is not only within each element, it is also "the domain of attractions center to center, that is to say, of convergence and union" (UP, Cuénot,2/Jan/53). It is "an autonomous power of organisation" active "in separate souls to orient and group them" (J,148). It has been present since the beginning of creation acting like a magnetic field which draws scattered elements together; it is the reverse gravity presented in Chapter One; it is "a synthesizing and directing energy, that stirs up and impels creatures towards a higher state of unity—something more like a spirit" (W,182). The conflicts of war are only the tribulations of ascent as love energy draws the human masses to form a psychic whole.

When Teilhard speaks of energy he would seem to have the following triadic schema in mind:

				Example 1	Example 2
Radial Energy,	Love: Soul	Consciousness	Freedom	The Cell	Unanimity
Tangential Energy,	Structure	Complexity	Determinism	The Crystal	Collectivity
Entropy,	Matter	Disorder	Chance	Individual Molecules	Individual Persons

This energy triad can be found on many levels: consider Example I. At a low evolutionary level, individual molecules (bottom of triad in Example I) are scattered in chance distribution. These molecules can come together in two ways: First, to form a *crystal* (tangential energy "links the element with all others of the same order"); this gives a more or less rigid structure that obeys the laws of determinism. But the molecules can also come together to form the centered and flexible living *cell* and so rise in radial energy. The same triad can be found at a higher level of the evolutionary scale (Example 2): human individuals (bottom of triad in Example 2) are somewhat unpredictable (chance). By forming a totalitarian *collectivity* they can be built into a rigid order that can be controlled almost mechanically. But beyond this they can gather in a loving *unanimity* that brings each to a sense of his own freedom. In each case, there is "chance at the bottom and freedom at the top" (P,308).

Each individual person is a "radial nucleus of consciousness" that faces an external world that he or she finds partially structured and partially a matter of chance ("fragments of a broken mirror"). Each individual instinctively feels a challenge to build this world; this would mean taking what one chances to find and using it to further order the world (increase the tangential energy—"repair the mirror"). By one's work in construction, industry, commerce and so forth, one is increasing order and thus tangential energy. And in working with the physical world (or the world of knowledge) one becomes aware that one is thereby deepening his or her personal identity, that is, deepening his or her radial energy. The ordinary way of developing oneself is by working with matter; Teilhard terms this process "the radial function of the tangential" (P,270). Since tangential development brings radial increase, the three stages of the energy triad are involved: through what one *chances* to find, one builds up *tangential* structures and therein one develops as a *radial* person. In no way does Teilhard explain why developing the tangential should increase the radial. Rather, he finds it an evident fact of experience: productive work is the ordinary way of developing oneself. Thus one needs a partially stubborn and disordered world as a challenge—without such a world there can be no personal growth. Chance is part of the process. Each element is:

> immersed in chance, it behaves there as though it were in a nutritive
> medium, choosing, seizing hold of and actively incorporating . . .
> it seeks to rise up radially, like a rocket (AE,107).

We must seize "every chance that comes our way" and draw from it all that we can; it is the only way that new elements can be introduced into our world and the only way that our spirits can rise. Thus, the opportunities of the material world are our nourishment ("by matter we are nourished"; it is "the food that nourishes" D,106,111). Thus, Noogenesis is said to rise "across the play of chance" (Lf,138). In terms of descent and ascent: we must leave the wholly structured world and descend to the world of chance (take some risk) or we will never rise up in spirit (the radial). The scientist must put his or her hypothesis to the test, and in doing so may find that the hypothesis does not hold; but this is the only way that his or her understanding can grow.

When the radial is increased, the process does not end, for the increased radial energy "will then be able to react in its turn in the form of a new arrangement in the tangential field. And so on" (P,65). Thus, the process becomes continuous: "a double movement which is one and the same." The individual "centers itself further on itself by penetration into a new space (a rise in radial) and at the same time it centers the rest of the world around itself" (P,172; parenthesis added). That is, as one deepens as a person he or she is better able to build the objective world.

What is true for the individual is true for Mankind. As individuals build a more extensively organized earth through technology and the common perspective of science, they begin to sense in themselves the growth of a common spirit. Thus, Teilhard would speak of "civilization spiritualizing by petrol" (Lf,29). Petrol does not become spirit: one is tangential and the other is radial. But the common spirit of Mankind rises in function of physical resources; this is again "the radial function of the tangential." When Teilhard worked with others in the physical sciences, he sensed a common spiritual bond drawing them together. From this he would argue that when all people devote themselves to building the earth (tangential) a common human bond will draw them together (radial). It is through building a common body that one develops a common soul. "Expansion in space and increased depths of spirit"; these are the "two conjoint movements" by which the common soul of mankind is developed (HE,137). There is a sequence: the physical world is developed through technology (or the theoretical world through science), and this leads to a common human spirit.

Men and women must come together not only *corps à corps* (through technology), nor *tête-à-tête* (through science), but *coeur à coeur* (through religion) (F,78). The final union can be realized only in function of a growth in body and mind; this is the radial function of the tangential.

It is only in the recent past that man has come to see that he himself is part of a world in process; now he is coming to see that he must assist in his own genesis (F,105). The new vision requires that man adopt a new morality: the morality that develops human energy. When the universe was thought to be a balanced structure, moralities were moralities of balance. They dealt with "a fixed system of rights and duties intended to establish a static equilibrium"; people were even urged to take the safer position (this was called "tutiorism"). But when people see that they are part of a developing universe they sense a goal to the process and begin to envision a new morality that will lead the universe to fulfillment. Now the moralist must become "the technician and engineer of the spiritual energies of the world" (HE,106). His aim is not to protect but to develop the world's potential and so assure "the release of every possible energy in it" (LT,164). The morality of property had been based on a stable system of exchange; now it must be based on "the idea of energy in movement" (HE,107). The morality of sexuality had been based on the maintenance of a stable society, now it must be a guide to help us master the terrifying energy present in sex. The truly moral man or woman of tomorrow will set out to explore "the mysterious ocean of moral energies"; and will "try everything and force everything in the direction of the greatest consciousness" (HE,108). Life has always been "an adventure, a groping, a risk," and this is what it must be today. And for this adventure the moralist must sense the direction and chart the path.

When Teilhard speaks of life as "an adventure, a groping, a risk" that needs direction, he is touching again on the fundamental movement of life: groping. Groping was defined as *directed chance,* a notion that now can be considered more fully. In any groping (exploration, research, etc.) one does not simply take chances and have experiences indiscriminately. To grope one must act with a goal, a direction, an intention. It is while retaining this intent that one opens himself up to experience. Thus groping (the basic movement of life) was defined as a composite of direction and chance (P,110), and thus involves the two foci of the soul, the two stars of Chapter Three. Direction refers to the *intent* towards the personal God, and chance to the more or less disordered chaos of experience. In order to grope, both stars are needed.

Teilhard had presented the two stars in terms of a geometrical image: one star was the center and the other was the circumference of a circle or a sphere. The image was developed in the previous chapters and is implied again in the terms "tangential" and "radial." Since each man or woman is a "radial center of consciousness," the human person could be represented (see figure 5) as a center, A, of a small sphere (his or her individual body, and *cogitata*). The surface of the sphere is the world insofar as it is centered around him; it is an individual's body and the ideas that he or she

animates. Tangential to the sphere is the plane NOP. The tangential
energies of this plane link physical matter into a system of determinisms
that are indifferent to any center. This is the impersonal universe that can
frighten us by its vast extent, it would be the blind determinism of matter
which would threaten to rule our lives. Beyond this plane is the random
flow of events, chance. The sphere is constituted by a small personal zone
of order (logic, theology, etc.). At O, the end of the radius AO,
experience seems to tell of a mixture of chance and determinism (both
seem far removed from any theology). Perhaps the individual will ignore
experience as best as he can. But the material world is insistent. It has
been revealing itself increasingly since the Age of Discovery and has
repeatedly forced man to widen his understandings of the world and of
himself.

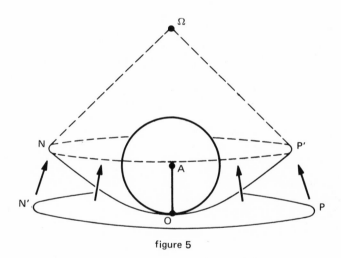

figure 5

In perception Teilhard would insist that the action is on the part of the
material world: it is the All that "forces itself inexorably on our attention"
(C,63), "the whole makes itself directly manifest to us . . . it almost
intuitively forces itself upon us" (C,58); it "reveals itself" to us (C,60); "it
is not that I have laboriously discovered the Whole, it is the Whole that
has presented itself to me, imposed itself on me" (C,43–44). Under the
impact of this imposition the individual might respond in two ways, both
of which are inappropriate: one might try to dissolve his or her radial
center in the Whole and thus achieve Nirvana; or one might do the reverse

and guard his or her radial center against all further intrusions of experience ("phenomena are an illusion"), and this is the way of the Yogi. These two ways reintroduce the conflict of two stars that has become familiar in this study. Teilhard had proposed that the two stars come together in conjunction; this occurs through two alternating movements: *perception* and *action*. In perception the Whole enters into the radial center of the perceiver: in action the radial center comes out of itself to impose its personal order on the universe. It is only through actively involving oneself in events that one finds his or her perception of events is heightened: things take on a sharpness of meaning only when we act upon them. The initially vague contours of reality take on form as we struggle with them (C, 103). Teilhard compares the process to the way that the sea will light up under the impact of a swimmer; so it is that matter is seen to light up with meaning and with the divine presence only under the impact of the person who struggles with it (D, 118;HU, 63).

To describe man's involvement with the earth, Teilhard would repeatedly use the image of Jacob wrestling with the angel (HU, 27;J, 11/ Sept/49;W, 14;D, 74). Jacob ends up adoring what he was struggling against. This image is basic to Teilhard's imaginative essay, "The Spiritual Power of Matter." Matter forces itself upon an individual and challenges him to respond. As they wrestle "the dark power wrestling with the man lit up with a thousand sparkling lights under the impact of his onslaught." There is a "reciprocal awakening of their opposed powers." The individual feels an increase of strength going out from him to balance the strength of the tempest, and from the tempest there comes forth in return a new exaltation which flows like fire in his veins (HU, 63). This exchange could be identified in several ways: it is the individual attempting to center the tangential about himself, in the process of which his own center is deepened; or it is the individual assembling the pieces of a broken mirror, and in the process being filled with light. Man succeeds in partially centering the world, but in the process the world gives the individual some of its tangential energy. This tangential quality stretches the small circle of personal identity to include all things; at that moment one feels within himself a deeper Self.

The whole image of perception and action tells of research. The researcher has a rational schema that he or she tries to impose on experience, but, generally, experience broadens the rational schema and the researcher as well (see D, 109). Finally the researcher himself becomes involved body and soul in the network of relationships that he or she had tried to cast on things from the outside. Both the world and the researcher have changed:

> A geologist would use the terms metamorphism and endomorphism. Object and subject marry and mutually transform each other in the act of knowledge; and from now on man willy-nilly finds his own image stamped on all he looks at (P,32).

Knowledge is a transformation of both object and subject, and that is what must characterize any mysticism of knowledge. The person who is seeking Nirvana is trying to become *pure object* by dissolving into the phenomena; the Yogi rejects objective phenomena and tries to retire into being purely a *subject*. Again the dilemma of the two stars, but now they can be identified as two mysticisms of *not-knowing*. One tries to become an object with no subject and the other a subject with no object. In either case there is no knowing. It is research that offers a third alternative: in research object and subject "wrestle" with each other; then "object and subject marry and mutually transform each other in the act of knowledge." Research is the process wherein the two stars come into conjunction; but in coming together they both become irrevocably different.

The process of research has two phases: *perception* and *action*. It is in perception that the All (random or tangential) imposes itself on the subjective center; it is in action that the subjective center imposes itself on the objective All. Perception and action is the two-fold movement of research and the two-fold movement by which life has been *groping* since the beginning as "directed chance"; in perception one opens oneself to what *chances* to be there; in action one orients what is there along a *direction*. This is the groping movement of life, and it is especially the movement of reflective life. Thus, man in his groping is the movement by which the two stars come together. Life itself has been characterized by a two-fold movement, a need "to perceive and act" (V,71); but non-reflective life formed only a "diffuse circle of perceptions and activities" (P,165). The double movement is properly found in reflective life (Thought): Man is "a center of perception and action" (J,172); "an independent center of perspective and activity" (D,141); "a center of perspective and action" (HE,100); "a nucleus for vision and action" (HE,142); he is involved in a "plurality of . . . perceptions and activities" (HE,154); seeking a "more direct mode of perception and action" (HE,130). This double process by which conjunction is effected would also characterize Mankind: men are "innumerable centers of perspective and action" (S,13, translation amended) developing "our common vision of the world and our common power of action," in a "neo-milieu of vision and action" (HM,87), by "a pan-human effort of investigation and construction" (P,249), "a total human act of vision and operation" (HM,86, transl. of final phrase amended). The alternation of perception and action turns out to be a "vast two way movement of ascent and descent" (see S,59). The stars are coming together. Object and subject are being married. In terms of an image from geology, through perception the world is endomorphizing the human person and through action the human person is metamorphizing the world.

In "The Spiritual Power of Matter" the wrestling individual became aware that the meaningless variations of the terrain passed away as the distant line of the horizon rose higher in the sky until the individual saw "himself standing in the center of an immense cup, the rim of which was closing over him" (HU,65). In the geometrical drawing previously shown the cup would be the cup-like N'OP' whose rim is continuing to mount and will eventually form a vast sphere. The tangential energies of the earth have become circumferential ("material energies of the earth will circulate"—HE,38); "the Divine Milieu should close around our lives like a circle" (D,138); the screen of the world "wraps itself in folds around us" (C,77); "I am encircled by its power, it seeks to close around me" (W,215). Becoming a circumference means that the tangential determinisms of matter have become centered to form a vast living Body. The wrestling individual feels he is swept by a mighty wind "which was sweeping the universe onwards." At the Center towards which the wind is moving a Being appears like the rising Sun: it is God "shining forth from the summit of matter whose waves were carrying the spirit to Him" (transl. amended). All things are seen to be filled with the divine presence for all is now His Body.

It was only through the incursions of matter that the individual began to respond and so came out of his or her own small center, A, into the vast universe and its Center, Omega. The individual had begun by trying to center the world around him or herself; matter resisted, and by resisting enlarged the circle of the individual's vision so that he or she came to see matter centering itself around a center deeper than the individual could call his or her own. The tangential plane cups to eventually form a sphere. From the luminous inner surface of the sphere (the screen or veil of phenomena) energy pours along radii to converge at the Center. This energy is the Flux of Convergence, the "great winds of cosmogenesis" (HM,98), the winds of Becoming. It is the flow of radial energy returning to its source; "the organizing energy of the mystical Body" (D,79); "the breath of a great wind" (HE,80); "a wind of the Spirit" (HE,54); coming in "great waves from the obscure places of the world" (HE,32). It is "the great wind of the social awakening of human consciousness" (HE,170); "a wind greater than we, coming we know not whence, passes through our soul" (HM,191); and in so doing draws all souls together in a vast "conspiration" (HE,37;V,60). It is love energy uniting humankind; it is the gaze of God (D,128). It is the world *rising* into the eyes of Christ, revealing itself in a great *perception*. When God *acts* upon the world, this is his *descent*. In *action* followed by *perception* it is the "world's essential energy" that first "radiates from this goal and finally flows back towards it" (see HE,145).

It is through our human gestures that the divine power radiates down through us to continue the creation of the great Body; this is the work of human action. Then the world lights up and radial energy reflects back through us into God; this is human perception. In every act of knowing the object and subject are said to marry. God has espoused matter, and sainted souls are said to become the brides of Christ (HM,66;T,65). We are changed by the marriage—but so is God. "All around us, and within our own selves, God is in the process of "changing," as a result of the coincidence of his magnetic power and our own Thought" (HM,53). The change takes place "all around us and within our own selves"; that is, it takes place at F,G,H,I, and A,B,C,D respectively in the drawing from the previous chapter. Now we can speak of the "complexity of God" (HE,68), for:

> . . . as God "metamorphized" the World from the depths of matter to the peaks of Spirit, so in addition the World must inevitably and to the same degree "endomorphize" God. As a direct consequence of the unitative process by which God is revealed to us, he in some way "transforms himself" as he incorporates us (HM,52–53).

The world is changed "from the depths of matter to the peaks of Spirit" (again F,G,H,I, and A,B,C,D). The world has been impressed with the image of the Knower to become his cosmic and mystic Body. But at the same time the divine Knower has been changed in his perception. He has "revealed" himself to us, and in being known He is no longer pure Subject. God has been "endomorphized" so that now he sees with the eyes of Christ.

Diminishment: Passivity in Action

In March of 1934 Teilhard was doing scientific work in China when a friend and scientific associate, Davidson Black, was found dead on the floor of their common laboratory. Teilhard and other co-workers were stunned by the event; it seemed to belie their common ideal of progress through building the earth. Teilhard reflected:

> what an absurd thing life is, looked at superficially: so absurd that you feel yourself forced back on a stubborn, desperate faith in the reality and survival of the spirit. Otherwise—were there no such thing as spirit, I mean—we should have to be idiots not to call off the whole human effort. . . . Black was the companion of my mind and my heart, and it was with him that I envisaged my work. But there is more in it than that. I mean a sharp and concrete realisation of the utter vanity of 'human effort' unless there is a both natural and supernatural emergence of the universe towards some immortal consciousness. In my distress following Black's death, and in the stifling atmosphere of 'agnostic' condolences that surrounded it, I swore to myself, on the body of my dead friend, to fight more vigorously than ever to give hope to man's work and inquiry (LT,202).

Teilhard's agnostic friends worked with an innate sense that the natural movement of the universe was going somewhere and they had dedicated themselves to further the process. But in each human death one of the finest products of progress decays, and, ultimately, the law of entropy assures us that the earth itself will likewise decay. When considering the universality of death, dreams of human progress are hollow and agnostic condolences are of little avail. For the human enterprise to make any sense at all one must believe in "the reality and survival of spirit," an "emergence of the universe towards some immortal consciousness."

Teilhard shared with his scientific associates a common belief in progress, but as a believing Christian he affirmed that with the phenomenon of death the reality of life continued. Thus, Teilhard would speak of a "double work" for the Christian: first, there is the work of prolonging natural evolution through involvement, a work Teilhard could share with his agnostic friends; then, there is the "work of detachment in God" (J,147), a work Teilhard could share with his Christian friends. Though one is attachment and one is detachment these two works, or rather, two stages or phases of a single work, are not opposed. They proceed in continuity with each other, they often alternate in the course of one's life. The significant difference between them is that the first is evident in the phenomenal world while the second is not—at least not directly. "The first phase is one of a *certain attachment to the world, a certain immersion* in the universe" (W,259). For this phase "science, the arts, industry, social activity" have their necessary part to play towards human development. We must build the earth and thereby develop a vigorous self.

This dynamic was treated in the previous section and is perhaps the best known theme in the writings of Teilhard. But as the individual proceeds towards a full human development of his powers, he gradually becomes aware of something new arising within himself: "The form it takes is *predilection for detachment*" (W,260). That is, one who is dedicated to the task of building the earth finds that an altruism and self-detachment begin to develop within. Such a person soon disregards anything that is petty, and, becoming aware of the really insurmountable barriers of physical life, such a person begins to long for the death that will bring relief. When the soul has taken its fill of the universe, it begins to find itself possessed by an intense need to die and leave its own self behind. "So begins the second stage of the soul's formation: the stage of *detachment* or of *emergence* from the world" (W,261). This is the moment of the *specifically* Christian operation: Christ empties man of the last of his egotism and takes his heart to replace it with his own. "He must increase, I must decrease." Perhaps one's body and one's mind begin to deteriorate. It is a grievous hour for the purely natural man, for the world and self that he had labored to build are giving way to the forces of diminishment. But it is an hour of deliverance for the man with faith in a transcendent God; for he believes that by the diminishment God is drawing him out of his material matrix and into Himself.

Often the two phases of attachment and detachment are fused into a single disinterested effort, but generally the first phase predominates in one's youth: one must "take possession of the world *in order to be*." Later one finds that he or she is quietly being possessed by a desire for detachment and death "for the sake of *being in another*" (D,96). Perhaps the phases alternate many times in the life of an individual. They have alternated many times in the life of the Church. Sometimes the Church has been very involved in human development, and sometimes it has withdrawn and preached a strict asceticism. Today, certain activist philosophies err in presenting only the first phase, as though the kingdom of God were wholly immanent to this world; but, conversely, some overly ascetic forms of Christianity have told only of the detachment (D,110). For Teilhard both phases are necessary, and further, both constructive effort and mystical *annihilation* "proceed from a single interior orientation." The same law regulates "the double movement of the natural personalization of Man and his supernatural depersonalization in Christ" (Li,35). Though both phases proceed from a single orientation, the difference between them suggests again the two stars: action-involvement tells of the descent, but in the involvement itself the reversal begins and one gradually draws away from matter. This is still the natural phase. The continuity of orientation is that the deepening (raising) of oneself that is part of the natural process is continued beyond apparent diminishment by a supernatural process. Both processes are part of a single journey into the divine Center.

The movement to God is both natural and supernatural and the continuity is that both have the same orientation—they both move back along the radius of the sphere. The previous section told of this movement as a wind rising from the lowest parts of the earth; it is the rising spirit of earth that develops through creative work. The movement arises as a function of physical growth but it can reach its term only through diminishment and death. Teilhard explains:

> I do not attribute any definitive or absolute value to the varied constructions of nature. What I like about them is not their particular form, but their function, which is to build up . . . what can be divinized . . . (D,93;Li,34).

The "varied constructions of nature" would refer to both the surrounding world and one's physical body. These develop through human work. But they have no "definitive or absolute value" for they will perish. They will give way to entropy. But they do have a "function": the radial function of the tangential. It is the rising radial energy of the "within" that will be divinized, while the tangential (through which the radial has risen) will fall back into the decay predicted by the physicists. Complexity and consciousness had developed together during the course of evolution, but, as indicated in Chapter One, they will separate to give a thinking without a brain. Therein the specifically Christian part of the work takes place; consciousness will continue to rise beyond its natural dependency upon material structure. The radial will no longer rise in function of the tangential but rather in function of God's direct action; one is no longer nourished by matter but rather is nourished directly by God. But the movement will be continuous for "the supernatural awaits and sustains the progress of our nature" (D,101).

When we first feel the forces of diminishment we must work against them with all of our might. It is only by opposing these forces that our spirit can make its natural rise. This is the natural development that Christians must share with all men. But however fine our opposition, the forces of diminishment will eventually gain mastery over the forces of life and will gradually drag us, physically vanquished, to the ground. A time will come when we must leave the world of appearances, the phenomenal world, make an "agonizing flight from the experiential zones," and pass "beyond the frontiers of the sensible world" (D,103). But we should not try to leave the material-phenomenal world in any premature way (D,107;F,52). Our departure must be in continuity with the world's development. This development has always been an arduous and painful task; this is how we have grown. But beyond this, Teilhard would refer to the road of human growth as "the royal road of the Cross," and see the whole human struggle resembling nothing so much as the way of the Cross (D,103;P,313). Spirit rises only by a laborious ascent; it continues, often in the face of overwhelming affliction; it finally arrives at what is often a painful death. "In this world . . . we are on the Cross" (W,67).

Teilhard found that in Christian preaching the Cross was often presented as a symbol of sadness and defeat, or even a symbol of God's rejection of human progress. Presented this way the Cross seems to go "against the current of man's aspirations and energies" (D,102,51). For Teilhard the Cross is rather the symbol of the immense labor of the centuries that little by little and at great sacrifice has raised up the human spirit. The movement of life is further like the Cross for it will appear to be a failure; success comes only in rising beyond death. Thus everyone who believes that "the vast movement and agitation of human life" is going to reach its goal, is one who believes in the Cross. The special power of the Cross turns human suffering and defeat—what would otherwise be only a great mass of debris—into a storehouse of treasure (W,67–68). The Cross is the symbol and the sign of evolution itself, for it tells of "the emergence of spirit across the play of chance" (Lf,142).

Those who are ill in body or mind find that they have a cross to bear in a special way. They often seem afflicted with useless pain and feel they are "cast up by the great stream of life, lying by sheer ill-luck incapable of work or activity." They seem to lack all meaning in a world of action and progress. Teilhard would urge them to see life in its totality as a single unified movement groping its way. In order to build the earth Life has had to take its chances, to risk, and thus inevitably some of the living will lose. Progress is being made, but only at great expense. Those who suffer are paying the price for the advance of the whole: "they are casualties, fallen on the field of honor," they are "like soldiers who fall during the assault which leads to peace" (HE,50;D,85). If we have to suffer we find ourselves asking, "Why me?" But the elements of life are not transposable at will; each is an integral part of the organic whole. In a bouquet the flowers have been artificially arranged, and a withered flower looks out of place; but on a large tree any withered flower is seen as integral to the life of the tree. This wider vision of life as a single organism can help the suffering individual gain a first understanding of his suffering. It is available to the natural man and woman. But if the suffering individual is a believing Christian he or she can enter in a special way into the second phase of the "double work." They who suffer are specially entrusted:

> with the task of sublimating and spiritualizing the general work of progress and conquest. . . . It is for them to stretch up to the divine more deliberately and more purely than the rest. It is for them to bring aid to their brothers who are working like miners in the bowels of matter (HE,50).

The Church is seen to be like a great tree, its roots are anchored in the bowels of matter, from matter it receives its nourishment and sap; but high above, the branches are oriented towards the sun and so refine and turn into flowers the sap extracted from the humblest roots (D,97,101, 107). Again the two stars: the roots are *nourished* by matter and the branches are *directed* towards the sun. The special function of the top is "to stretch up to the divine more deliberately and more purely" in order that the final phase of the double work might be accomplished. Through their *intent* in the midst of suffering and though they are "the humblest of patients," (that is, they are passive) their suffering is transformed "into a supremely active principle of universal hominisation and divinisation" (AE,248).

Though they have been rendered passive, they are still "supremely active." This activity is the supernatural rise of the radial continuing within a human soul oriented towards God. In the one who is suffering "the ascending force of the world is concealed in a very intense form" (HE,51). Thus, the Cross of Christ is said to be "the symbol and place of an action whose intensity is beyond expression" (HE,52). It is on the Cross that the second phase of the work is being accomplished; there Jesus is bringing into God "the advances of the universal march" (HE,52; transl. amended).

Teilhard would link the "activity" of the ill with the "activity" of the contemplatives within the Church. Contemplatives resemble the sick in that they do not labor "in the bowels of matter"; they too stretch more purely towards God; they have an "inward tension of the mind towards God." But they too are not simply passive. If one could see what is really taking place, the soul of a contemplative would appear "active in this world, by virtue of its sheer purity" (D,134). The outstanding contemplative is seen to be the Virgin Mary; by the purity of her intent towards God she exemplifies "passive action" (MM,149). Teilhard would insist, "Purity, in spite of outward appearances, is essentially an active virtue."

The ideal of "passive action" has a long tradition in the writings of the mystics. It obviously relates to the *"in nobis sine nobis"* treated in the previous chapter. To understand its unique meaning in the writing of Teilhard one must consider Teilhard's repeated identification of man as a center of *perception* and *action* (previous section). Those who are contemplative, those who are ill, and Jesus on the Cross have one thing in common: they do not themselves *act* on the world in any significant way. But they do continue to *perceive,* that is, they contemplate. But, as was shown in the previous section, in perception there is an action; it is on the part of the object perceived: it is the All that "reveals itself," or "imposes itself." The contemplative does not actively wrestle with matter; the contemplative withdraws insofar as this is possible from the course of world events; he takes fewer chances. These do not nourish him; in function of them his radial energy does not rise. But still he is not simply passive. Rather in his apparent passivity, he is the place of intense activity; though he himself does not act, the action of contemplation is entirely on the part of the object. The contemplatives are passive and perhaps enduring a great suffering (they are *patientes*), but in them "the ascending force of the world is concealed in a very intense form." All that is given them to *do* is to orient this force, to give it *direction,* to "stretch up to the divine" more purely than the rest. They are pure perception, receiving in themselves the rising All of the universe; then by purity of intention the All passes through them to God. In their suffering passivity they are like Christ stretched on the Cross, while through them rises "the advances of the universal march." The universe has entered one focus of their soul ("that of experience") and passed out the other (the "purity of intention") to the revealed God. In them there is no descent (action); they are pure rise.

One day all the power in matter will be exhausted; then the descent of God to the world will have come to an end. But the ascent back to God will continue for a while. Humanity will become more contemplative; it will feel less need for earthly nourishment, and contemplation will gain mastery over anxious human work. All of the divine substance that has descended will have risen into the soul of humanity and humanity will be ready for the Parousia—the final great manifestation of God (D, 110).

In the first chapter of this study a text of Teilhard's later years was quoted wherein he identified the element that he had always been seeking: it was the Flux of Convergence. This Flux was seen to be only a clarification of other terms found throughout his earlier writings: transience, Spirit, the Becoming, radial energy. One's journey into God is not complete until one has become part of this stream. That is, the molecule of one's being must be broken and one must lose all immanence, become wholly transient, wholly spirit, wholly Flux. In short, one's being must be annihilated so that one can fully enter the Becoming. It is Spirit-Flux-Becoming that is divinizable and that will finally be divinized. It is through one's personal center that one remains apart from this movement. What is needed is a difficult phase of excentration. This is the work of suffering: those who suffer "are in a sense driven out of themselves" (HE, 50). But even their suffering is not enough: "there is a further step to take—the one that makes us lose all foothold within ourselves" (D, 88; W, 132). Before God can fill us he must empty us, "he must break the molecules of our being" (D,89). We must "lose our footing completely in ourselves" (W,132). Death allows God to enter into "our innermost hearts, in the last stronghold that might have escaped his reach" (D,82). It is not for ourselves that we enter into the final act, for by the final act we lose ourselves. We surrender and the world itself reaches its fulfillment. "The completion of the world is only consummated through a death, a 'night,' a reversal, an excentration, and a quasi-depersonalisation" (D,93). All of these fill the natural man with fear. But the mystic longs for death and excentration, for only thus can one become part of the divinizable spirit, the Flux of Convergence that God will divinize.

Chastity and the Ascent

Teilhard ends his brief autobiography (*The Heart of Matter*) with an extended note on the Feminine. He writes that from the time his own ideas began to take shape, he had no self-development "without some feminine eye turned on me, some feminine influence at work." The only thing he found unusual about this is that he did not encounter Woman until he was thirty years old and on the eve of going to war—probably a reference to meeting his cousin Marguerite in Paris. His wartime letters to Marguerite attest to her influence during this most creative period of his life. It was to her that he sent each of his wartime essays. Later, many other women would give him inspiration and encouragement; his friendships with them would continue until the day of his death. As he was Platonic in much of his thinking, he was also Platonic in his friendships; though he was endlessly fascinated by women, his relationships always seem to have been chaste.[1]

Teilhard would see the warmth and charm of women "absorbed drop by drop into the life blood" of his thought. Thus, his reflections on women would restate all the familiar themes of this study. In his first essay, the temptation of matter could equally have been called the temptation of women: Matter invites him to be lulled to sleep "by the great mother"; from the nether world rises the "song of the sirens"; matter is the "fertile generatrix," the "Terra mater," the "Temptress" inviting man to surrender "in a sort of sensual abandonment." Soon he realized that matter was bringing "dissolution in her train; her alluring face masked a lack of thought and an empty heart" (W,60). He rejects the temptation and commits himself to working with the upwards movement of life. The feminine aspect of the earth is seen to undergo a corresponding change: "the Mistress, ingratiating and yet dominating, has now been replaced . . . Matter is now the mysterious betrothed who is won, like the hunter's prey, in high combat" (W,32). As he makes his laborious ascent "the immanent Goddess of the World" ascends with him. Then he comes upon "the glittering gem of matter . . . Mary . . . the day of the Virgin came to pass" and from her the transcendent God is born (W,59). Thus, it was not just matter but Matter-Feminine that first lured Teilhard to shift the axis of his life outside himself and make the descent. When he made his reversal the Temptress became the betrothed—an image that implies abstinence until a final consummation—but finally it is the Virgin who leads him to communion with God.[2]

Teilhard's wartime Journal is filled with references to woman, sexuality, chastity and virginity. All the references are philosophical rather than personal. Shortly after completing his first essay he began writing an essay on woman-virginity. But it was almost two years before he finished a brief and highly imaginative work: "The Eternal Feminine." The essay is dedicated to Beatrice, the woman who inspired Dante. The allusion gives the key to Teilhard's essay; again there will be the descent and the ascent. Dante was drawn by his encounter with Beatrice out of his solitary complacency to make a troubled journey to the nether world and ascend by a laborious journey to Paradise where Beatrice greets him and again the Virgin directs him to God. Teilhard's "Eternal Feminine" is divided into two parts and the two parts recall the two stars.

In the essay the Feminine herself is the speaker. In the first part she identifies herself as the power present at the world's creation, the power that drew the atoms out of their solitude:

> I bestirred the original mass, almost without form . . . and I instilled even into the atoms, into the fathomless depths of the infinitesimal, a vague but obstinate yearning to emerge from the solitude of their nothingness and to hold fast to something outside of themselves (W,193).

Through the drawing power of the Feminine the atoms surrender their individuality (make their descent); then they are drawn into the first synthesis and thus the ascending process of life begins. The Feminine arouses the song of birds, the wild hum of insects and the blooming of flowers; now man is also feeling her power. At first man thinks he is reaching out to embrace another individual like himself, but is astonished by the violence of the forces unleashed within him. He has been drawn into the universal process of creation. He seeks for glory, power, or scientific truth, but through all of these he is being drawn by the magnetism of the Feminine. The Feminine explains: "I open the door to the whole heart of creation: I, the Gateway of the Earth, the Initiation" (W, 195). Just as matter is found to be ambiguous, so is woman; in her is knowledge of good and evil, in her is temptation and salvation. If man seeks only pleasure in woman he will disintegrate and embrace only dust; but it is also through woman that man might ascend to God.

The second part of the essay begins by citing the praise of virginity found in Christian revelation. Now woman is boundlessly idealized: "Henceforth my name is Virginity." But the Virgin is still woman and mother, she is mother Church and the Virgin Mary where heaven and earth are drawn together in passionate union. Now the Feminine promises, "Soon there will be nothing but God for you in a Universe entirely virginized" (W, 200, transl. amended). When the divine union is complete, the feminine image will play over the surface of the divine fire and remain still as Eternal Feminine. Thus the Feminine turns out to be a heavenly Form that is reflected throughout the earth and which begins the unifying process.

The essay also made use of an unusual term, "virginized." This and related terms (*virginizé, virginization*) occur frequently in Teilhard's early Journal (74,76,77,78,83,etc.) In these passages Teilhard is trying to reconcile the natural development of the earth with Christian Revelation. The Revelation commends virginity (see I Cor.7:38;Matt.19:11) and Teilhard was particularly conscious of this because of his religious vows. At the same time it is evident that evolution has not been proceeding by virginity. Teilhard's solution would involve an analogy: just as evolution entered a new phase with the appearance of thought—but a new phase in continuity with what had proceeded—so now evolution was entering another new phase with the appearance of virginity, and once again there would be a continuity. "Virginity rests upon chastity as thought upon life" (T, 85). Chastity refers to the limited use of sexual expression that characterizes many good marriages. By this restraint the couple would often grow as persons. In virginity this restraint would become total so that personal growth could reach fulfillment. Thus, to reach its term in God, mankind would ultimately "virginize."

When Teilhard first proposed the "double work" of attachment and detachment (treated in previous section) he identified the second phase, detachment, as "virginisation" (J,147). This second phase was seen to continue the growth of the universe but no longer by the radial function of the tangential; the radial growth was continued by the direct intervention of God. In terms of virginity Teilhard is saying that for ages humanity sublimated the tangential attraction of sex into spiritual growth; now God will continue this radial growth apart from tangential contact. In terms of the drawing presented at the end of the previous chapter, we move closer to Ω by our tangential involvement (A to B), that is, by our involvement with another individual. But the final movement from B to Ω takes place without a tangential contact. Thus in the end there will be nothing but God "in a Universe entirely virginized."

During the 1930s chastity again became a personal concern for Teilhard; it was often treated in his essays and letters and he assures us that he was not writing "monologues in abstracto" (Li,263). In 1934 he completed "The Evolution of Chastity" and explained in a covering letter: "It is the best I could tell myself and the other when three or four times in my life for long periods I was up against the wall" (Li,275). Chastity brings with it certain tensions, but life itself is a "tense current" moving away from the relaxation of matter. Teilhard speaks of difficult times he has had with chastity, but what is of real significance for him is that he does not thereby feel personally impoverished. During the 1930s Teilhard's writings centered on the dynamics of energy, and it was in this context that he considered human love and the awesome energies involved. He would see the world possessing a certain quantum of energy, but through humans not knowing how to love this energy was being dissipated in a terrible waste (HE,34). That is, when one loses himself in the enjoyment of physical possession he undergoes "a lapse into plurality and return to nothingness." This wastage is identified as the "true explanation of the disorders of impurity" (HE,75). Teilhard had not yet developed his radial and tangential terminology but it is implicit in what he writes. He tells of descending in order to ascend, immersion in order to emerge, and tells of the need to share in things in order to carry them along: "the energy which fuels our interior life . . . is in its primitive roots of a passionate nature" (T,68).

Thus one descends to the tangential energy of passion in order that spirit might rise along the radial. This presents a basic problem: one might argue that the flame that appears in sexual union leaps upward to God. If this were so, then full sexual expression would have "the advantage of most fully releasing, for God, the spiritual potentialities of passion" (T,83). Teilhard would not want to say this. But even the phrase, "the spiritual potentialities of passion," suggests an obvious parallel with "the radial function of the tangential." Because of this parallel one might argue for frequent sexual encounters in order to develop one's radial person: "To maintain the drive of spirit, fill up with fuel!" (T,69). But though there is some parallel with this line of his thought Teilhard had a weighty reservation: in the very intensity of sexual expression

> a sort of 'short-circuit' is produced in the dazzling gift of the body—a flash which burns up and deadens a portion of the soul. Something is born, but it is for the most part used up on the spot. What constitutes the peculiar intoxication that comes with complete giving may very well be that in it we burn away part of our 'absolute' (T,84).[3]

Teilhard is allowing that in the intensity of sexual union passion (tangential energy) does give rise to spirit (radial), but this radial is immediately consumed. Therefore he would suggest: "No immediate contact, but convergence at a higher level" (T,84).

In the previous section Teilhard was seen to speak of two phases in human work: first, a phase of involvement with the world, and then a phase of detachment and emergence. In 1916 when he first outlined the two phases in his Journal he seems to have been more concerned with the nature of sexuality than with human work. He identified the second phase as "virginisation" (J,147). He added that the two phases were generally found in each individual, but this would not always be the case: some are called to the more specialized state of marriage and some to the more specialized state of the mystic. Thus, virgins and contemplatives would specialize in the second phase of the work. Teilhard would introduce the same two phases in "The Evolution of Chastity" and use them to explain a transformation he saw presently taking place in human love: "Love is going through a 'change of state' in the noosphere" (T,86). Love is moving increasingly into the second phase. In the future lovers will turn away from the body and seek one another more directly in God. Just as he would envision involvement in the world eventually giving way to increased contemplation, so he would see sexual expression increasingly giving way to virginity. There would still be a tangential component as one would still feel a passionate attraction for the opposite sex (S,76). But one would "sublimate" passion in order that his spirit might rise. Since passion is still involved there would still remain much of the dynamic of the first phase: the radial function of the tangential.

Heretofore, the primary institutionalized way of dealing with sexuality has been marriage; a second institutionalized way has been through the celibacy of the more or less complete separation that characterizes religious life. Teilhard would propose what he would term a third way: As in marriage two individuals would come together to form a paired unit. (Spirituality is not to be found so much in the single individual as in the human dyad. T,71;HM,60,80) The man and woman would energize one another and draw one another forth, but they would remain virgin. For the further development of Mankind, it is not a question of eliminating human passion, but of getting control of passion so that it might serve spirit. Thus, Teilhard would envision virgin couples becoming ever more common as chastity enters the next phase of its evolution. The physical energies of the earth have been brought under control and by the very process have increased the radial. Now the energies of passionate love must be brought under control and in the process raise the "affective dyads" into God.

The Mass on the World

Teilhard was always somewhat surprised to find others experience difficulty in conceiving of a personal God. He writes that throughout his life he never had the least difficulty in addressing himself to God as to a supreme Someone (HM,41). During his wartime service as he worked over thoughts of "vision and action," of "growth and diminishment," his thoughts began taking the shape of a prayer. He was in the forests about the Aisne River where the tall columns of trees arched over him in vaults of greenery and he could not imagine a better temple of recollection (MM,213). He did not have all that he needed to offer Mass, but he repeated some of the prayers of the Mass and gradually the prayers lent a pattern to his thoughts. He wrote his thoughts as a prayer in an essay called "The Priest." He asked that by his very priesthood he might henceforth be the first to become aware of what the world loves, pursues and suffers, "the first to seek, to sympathize, to toil: the first in self-fulfillment, the first in self-denial" (W,222). He finished the essay in July of 1918.

Teilhard made the first of many trips to China in 1923 and there he rewrote his reflections on the Mass and called it "The Mass on the World." As he surveyed the bad-lands of Mongolia and excavated Pliocene fossils from towering red cliffs, the texts kept going through his mind. "As I travel on mule back for whole days on end, I repeat, as in the past—for lack of any other Mass—the "Mass on the World" (LLZ,52). He never spent such care on a text. Years later he was "ceaselessly deepening and working over" the phrases trying to bring them to their final form. In the years before his death he made endless Journal notations for a final version that never appeared.[4]

In both the arching forests of the Aisne and the towering cliffs of Mongolia Teilhard was without the bread, the wine and the altar he needed for Mass. He was moved by all he saw around him to make the earth his altar and on it offer the labors and sufferings of the world. On his paten he would place the harvest that would grow in the world that day; in his chalice he would pour the sap that would be pressed painfully out of the earth's fruit. Thus, in the elements offered as "Mass" he introduces the two phases of the double work: *growth* (the bread) and *diminishment* (the wine). His paten and chalice are his own soul open wide to receive all that stirs in the dark heart of matter and the ocean of living humanity. The antagonisms of the surface fade in his perception so that he becomes aware of great rivulets of desire "flowing together in one common aspiration" (W,206). From the depths of the formless mass rises a hallowing cry of all creation speaking together: "Lord, make us one." Having "descended" to the unformed All he finds that it is rising in a "tense current" towards the unifying and transcendent God. He looks towards the revealed God (the other focus of his paten-chalice-soul) and makes the invocation of his priesthood:

> Over every living thing which is to spring up, to grow, to flower, to ripen during this day say again the words: This is my Body. And over every death-force which waits in readiness to corrode, to wither,

to cut down, speak again your commanding words which express the
supreme mystery of faith: This is my Blood (HU,23).

Through Christ's claiming all growth and all diminishment, the
double consecration, is effected and the converging world in all its
movements is filled with inner fire. The divine presence has invaded
everything from "within" and rendered it substantial. God is present all
around the priest. He responds in a prayer of adoration, but the process is
not complete. He is not simply to contemplate the divine presence in the
world, for he is a center of contemplation *and action*. He is to receive it
into himself in communion: "Faith consecrates the world. Fidelity
communicates with it" (D,138;LLZ,67;S,77). Now he must pass from
the vision of faith to the fidelity of action. The bread he must receive will
consist of all the forces that dilate the world; by acting in the world
Teilhard knows that he too will be dilated and torn painfully out of
himself and cast into danger and a constant renewal of ideas. But:

> The man who is filled with an impassioned love of Jesus hidden in
> the forces which bring increase to the earth, him the earth will lift
> up, like a mother, in the immensity of her arms, and will enable him
> to contemplate the face of God (HU,30).

Ultimately the Kingdom of God is not of this world, so communion
with God is not complete in a process of visible growth. The final term to
which the world is moving is beyond all phenomena, so it is only by
passing through an agonizing excentration, a collapse of everything that
looks like growth for himself and humanity that his communion can be
complete:

> If my being is ever to be decisively attached to yours, there must first
> die in me not merely the monad ego but also the world: in other
> words I must first pass through an agonizing phase of diminution for
> which no tangible compensation will be given me. That is why,
> pouring into my chalice the bitterness of all separations, of all
> limitations, and of all sterile fallings away, you then hold it out to
> me. 'Drink ye all of this.'

To communicate with God or to communicate with anyone will always
involve an act of surrender (HU,30;W,125,215;HE,155). By action

Teilhard spoke of passing out of himself. So by communion in action we are drawn out of ourselves into a common life that we cannot wholly control. Now this wider life of the universe in which our deeds share is seen by eyes of faith to be the life of Jesus. Teilhard quotes St. Gregory of Nyssa, "The bread of the Eucharist is stronger than our own flesh; that is why it is the bread that assimilates us, and not we the bread when we receive it" (S,76). By his Communion with God through faithful action Teilhard finds he is carried out of himself by a devouring power which "far from being consumed by me, consumes me" (D,126;HU,29); "the Bread . . . takes hold of me and draws me to itself" (W,215).

An individual can contemplate world events from a distance and see them comprising a consuming world process. He comes to see himself as an infinitesimal element in a vast torrent of energy pouring out of the darkness of the past. It was not his will that set the torrent in motion. Soon he must become again engaged in events and find their life will absorb his own. If he is a man of "natural" faith, he will believe that events are going somewhere and that by engaging with them he will commune in their common life. But again and again his faith will confront the absurdity of pain and death. If he is a man of Christian faith, he will still believe events are going somewhere and commune in their common life; but as a Christian he will believe that his communion will be complete only after a difficult phase of diminishment and death. By his own annihilation he is being drawn apart from the phenomena into the bosom of God.

Teilhard wrote his first reflection on the Mass as a prayer for ordained priests in time of war. When he rewrote the essay it was not clear for whom it was written. Gradually he extended its meaning until it became a prayer for all Christians who work to build the earth. In a special way it would be a prayer for all scientists: the believing scientist is "a sort of priest" (T,16); he participates "in the priestly function" (HE,179); "scientists are priests" (Lf,164,233). But this priesthood is present only insofar as one has faith. Through human faith the divine power descends to animate the world, this is the moment of Consecration. Through human fidelity the divine power rises back to God bringing the nourishment of matter back to God to complete his great Body; this is the moment of communion. The event can transpire in *Everyman*—provided he believe:

And thus in thee the circuit vast
Is rounded and complete at last,

And at last, through thee revealed
To God, what time and space concealed.

Teilhard would write many essays "as an attempt to see and to make others see." Both faith and knowledge are necessary for the great work to continue. Many scientists have no faith or keep their faith apart from their work; they engage in research only to find they are depersonalized by the work they do. Perhaps their work seems trivial and dull, so they turn to it with only half of their heart:

> That is why after a life of highest effort, a scientist or thinker may end up impoverished and dessicated—disillusioned; his mind but not his personality has worked on inanimate objects. He has given himself; he has not been able to love (HE, 147).

If faith is absent or if it is kept in an area apart from one's research, the world will appear empty and dead. One will deal with inanimate objects in an inanimate way. One's heart will be slowly consumed in a tiring routine and all the while one will wonder why he is burdened by an immense need to love. But once the world is lit by the vision of faith, Christ becomes present everywhere. Faith is an operative power! Everything is seen to move to a loving term and so is "warmed, illumined and animated." Now it is possible "to love (with real love, with a true love) the universe in process of formation" (T, 204). One can embrace the lowliest task with devotion, for everything one handles is a touch and a caress from God. In everything one encounters, one encounters his personal Lord; the believer "can give himself boundlessly to everything he does." Every event is different now, "the whole distance between consumption and communion" (HE, 148).

Teilhard first became a writer to testify to a Communion with God through Matter. This was the message of "Cosmic Life" and remained the whole of what he had to say. To enter the communion one first descends to the formless All and then reverses to rise with the ascending current of life. Filled with the immensity of the universe one becomes aware that all things form a converging torrent of desire calling out to God: "You are our Soul." This is the Offertory of Teilhard's Mass. There follows the consecration wherein God himself responds, "This is my Body." By the divine claim Body and Soul are joined together; that is, the universe assumes the Form of Christ. But soon the Christ is seen to be the Christ crucified. Over the crucible of the world's diminishment and pain the divine claim is repeated, "This is the Cup of my Blood." The risen Christ has come to fill all things as their Alpha and Omega,—as the first and the last—as the living, the dead and the risen again. Every object and every event has become hallowed. Now I can lovingly receive into myself the life of the universe, for I know that through everything that happens to me the loving God is drawing me into Himself. Now, nothing can separate me from the love of God, neither height nor depth, neither principality nor power, neither growth nor diminishment. Everything that happens has become the loving and adorable action of God—provided only that I believe. Faith is an operative power. Now the changes of fortune that will constitute my life or any life have become only the gently alternating phases of a Great Communion: in growth I commune with his Body, in diminishment I commune with his Blood.

During the course of his life Teilhard knew a success and growth that was more than ordinary: he was a co-discoverer of the Peking Man; he published hundreds of scientific articles; he received recognition and scientific honors. But during his life he also came to know a frustration and diminishment that was more than ordinary: the Jesuits and the Church forbade him to publish his philosophic and religious writings and he was finally sent to spend his last years away from the Paris he had loved. He was frail, old, and recovering from a coronary when he arrived in New York City. But all the pictures of him show that the fire still flashed in his eyes. He resumed his scientific work but again and again would write short testimonies to the Great Communion that had moved him to become a writer many years before. He knew the end would be coming soon and prayed that he might end well. Friends kept urging him to retain his priesthood but leave the Jesuits—for thereby he could publish. But Teilhard knew he must keep fidelity to the end; that alone made all things a Communion. He knew diminishments would come, but that they too were a part of what life is about. Many years before his final stay in New York he had written:

> When the signs of age begin to mark my body (and still more when they touch my mind); when the ill that is to diminish me or carry me

off strikes from without or is born within me; when the painful moment comes in which I suddenly awaken to the fact that I am ill or growing old; and above all at that last moment when I feel I am losing hold of myself and am absolutely passive within the hands of the great unknown forces that have formed me; in all those dark moments, O God, grant that I may understand that it is you (provided only my faith is strong enough) who are painfully parting the fibres of my being in order to penetrate to the very marrow of my substance and bear me away within yourself. . . . You are the irresistible and vivifying force, O Lord, and because yours is the energy, because, of the two of us, you are infinitely the stronger, it is on you that falls the part of consuming me in the union that should weld us together. . . . Teach me *to treat my death as an act of communion* (D,89–90).

Teilhard died suddenly on Easter Day, April 10, 1955.

Notes

Chapter 1

1. Teilhard was ambiguous in his use of the term "pantheism." Sometimes he would simply reject what it implies, at other times he would speak favorably of a "Christian pantheism."

2. Teilhard makes a number of confusing references to the date of the reversal. Thus, in August of 1929 he would write, "A first progress occurred in my soul fifteen years ago when I understood that . . . (Letter to E. LeRoy). In the same month he would write, "After spending some ten years over the simple reversal of views . . . now . . ." (LLZ,94).

3. Socrates dealt with the dilemma without much success in *The Parmenides;* he refused to discuss it in *The Theaetetus.* Plato would later introduce the Stranger into his dialogues. In *The Sophist* the Stranger would propose that in a sense non-being is and being is not. Teilhard would seem to follow in this tradition in allowing that matter is "positive non-being" (W,163). Because of his reversal Teilhard would come to a position that would have much in common with the Idealist tradition in philosophy; but his idealism was always moderated by the "positive" role he assigned to matter. Plato had posed the question: are the forms entirely distinct or do they "participate" in one another? For Teilhard matter is that which enables the forms to participate in one another. But Teilhard would warn that Matter itself does not unite; Matter serves only as hand-hold for union (*donne prise a l'union*, HM,227). This will be treated in Chapter Three when Teilhard's "trans-matter" spirituality is considered.

4. Teilhard would soon back away from this solution and propose instead that "another matter" would be given to the soul after death; this is what the soul would unify (J,200). Then in 1919 he would see these separated souls being given reconstituted or resuscitated matter, and similarly in 1920 (MM,236–37;Li,59). The issue can be better understood if reference is made again to the earlier diagram: there, F,G,H, and I would be the matter that falls away and is later reconstituted. Teilhard would develop a further terminology to deal with the double levels involved: Christ is said to have both a mystical and a cosmic Body (W,58,59,110,146,175,297;J,216). In the drawing, the mystical Body would be A,B,C,D,E (the souls of individuals united as spirit), while the cosmic Body would be F,G,H,I, etc.—after death this body would be composed of

reconstituted matter. Teilhard would write that "the mystical Body of Christ is haloed by a cosmic Body, that is to say, by *all things* in so far as they are drawn by Christ to converge upon him and so reach their fullness in the Pleroma" (W,297). In the drawing the mystical Body (A,B,C . . .) is seen to be haloed by the cosmic Body (F,G,H . . .). After 1920 Teilhard would drop all mention of reconstituted matter; he would likewise make no mention of the cosmic Body, though there would be a Cosmic Body of Christ as long as people continued to live on earth.

5. Several unpublished sources give dates that are of interest in tracing the development of Teilhard's thought:

> in August of 1929 he writes, ". . . a first progress occurred in my soul fifteen years ago when I understood that the consistence of the universe is "ahead in the Spirit," and not "behind in Matter"; a second step is now happening in me by the growing view that Spirit completes itself (consists) in personality (or ultra-personality)" (UP, E. LeRoy, 10/Aug/29).

During his annual retreat in June of 1952 he would write:

My great illuminations:

	0	The Milieu is a Center 1927 *The Divine Milieu.*
	1	Union differentiates (personalizes) (Peking '37).
cosmic	2	Complexity "engenders" consciousness (Peking '42).
function	3	Reflection increases. The step and the progresses of reflection (Peking—Nietzsche).
makes cosmic	4	(The convergence of the Universe) Evolution converges. The
(state)		convergence of the Universe (Retreat Notes).

Perhaps these dates should not be taken too seriously: Union differentiates is dated 1937. But in his Journal on Sept. 1916 he had written, the Monad "individualizes itself by integrating itself with the chosen all"; in March of 1918 he wrote of "unitive differentiation" (J,290), and in Feb. 1919 the Universal Element "unifies by differentiating" (W,301).

Chapter 2

1. A noted geneticist, Theodosius Dobzhansky, has adopted Teilhard's word, "groping," with enthusiasm. (*The Biology of Ultimate Concern,* p.114ff.).

2. Perhaps he even began keeping a journal to consider this problem (see J,20;MM,63,200). The relationship between progress and evil seems to have been the subject of an early essay now lost.

3. For example, in *Vision of the Past,* similar references to eyes occur on pp.8,13,22,26,42,43,51,etc. One seven-page essay in the same book has the following expressions: "the universe has appeared to human eyes," "takes shape before our eyes," "distinguishable to our eyes," "researchers' eyes," "beneath our eyes," "within vision of natural science" (V,238ff).

4. Darwin would seem to have made a similar observation when he noted that

it is easy "to admit in words the truth of the universal struggle for life," but "we do not see" or "dimly see" this struggle when we watch the song birds and flowers (Darwin, *Orig. of Species,* 116).

5. In general Teilhard was uninterested in spiritists, psychics and theosophists even though a number of his friends and associates had such an interest (Breuil, Valensin). Li, 109 quotes various comments of Teilhard in regard to psychics; in general, he objects that they mix the "spheres" of the real (a similar criticism is often made of Teilhard). During his latter years he was aware that a number of psychics had appealed to his writings to justify or explain themselves. But Teilhard would only say, "I avoid them like the fire" (UP,Mortier, 15/Mar/55). Cuenot quotes a Dutch parapsychologist who tells of Teilhard being familiar with the literature and the work of J.B.Rhine and C.G.Jung (Cuenot,312).

6. These two phrases occur in his Journal (15/Nov/52; 25/Mar/52). The latter reference reads "Platonicisme (*d. C . . .*) *evolutionisé*"; the parenthesis is in the text, it includes two words difficult to read, possibly they read *"du Coeur."* Teilhard had only a second-hand knowledge of Plato during WWI (MM,224), but later became more familiar with him. He would also express serious reservations about Plato (See J,16/Mar/55).

Chapter 4

1. Teilhard has abundant references to human isolation: each individual seems to be a "reflective monad" (AE,218), a "closed fragment following its own course" (F,95), "a closed unit" situated in a "throng of other units, equally locked in on themselves" (AE,68). There is misery in feeling "shut in, impenetrable to one another" (W,110); yet "our individual microcosms tend jealously to isolate themselves" (D,143), so that by "our solitary egoisms the universe is threatened with disintegration into a dust of separate freedom particles" (HE,75). In politics this "accentuation of psychic autonomy" has given rise to a "sharper sense of the rights of each unit"; but it has also resulted in a neglect of the common good. There is even a misguided morality of individualism that would suggest that a certain "rebellious independence" is the "ideal moral attitude" (V,140,265). Teilhard confessed to having such feelings himself (see D,145).

2. The reverse would also seem to be true: "the element only becomes personal when it universalizes itself" (P,263).

3. The section is titled *"L'Eveile Cosmique"* which the English renders as "Awakening to the Cosmos." This neatly misses the point of the section, for what Teilhard is saying is that the cosmos as Object known is awakening to itself as Subject knowing. *Sensation, Sens,* and *sentir* are key words for Teilhard, but in English the association of the terms is not evident; *sensation* is sometimes translated as feeling, sometimes as sensitivity, and sometimes as sensation. Even *"sens (et sentiment)"* is somehow rendered as "perception, intellectual and emotional" (HM,82). Teilhard would write that the *sens* of the divine presence is not the same as the *sentiment* of the same (see D,130).

4. In his latter years Teilhard considered it highly probable that there was reflective life elsewhere in the universe (CE,229ff;P,286). In his Journal he would

accordingly allow that R2 might include a second phase, *"Réflexion inter-planetaire"* (J,2/Jul/51). As early as 1925 Teilhard had linked revelation to reflection calling it "in some way a 'face' of reflection" (UP, E.LeRoy, 16/Aug/26). In 1929 he writes of "the reflection of the whole upon the monad—in other words, a revelation" (T,36). Revelation as ultra-reflection becomes a frequent theme in his Journal from 1951 until the time of his death (e.g. "the third reflection, it is not only the Revelation, but also the Incarnation" J,23/June/52). He wrote a letter telling of his intention to write an essay, "The Reflection of Energy" which would end with a section on "the third reflection: the reflection (revelation) of God on the Universe itself in the course of reflection (individual and total) upon itself" (Mortier, 10/Sep/51). But in writing the essay he finds it "not publishable as the third chapter contains a series of perspectives on the Supernatural and Revelation" (Mortier, 30/Nov/51). "Not publishable" refers to the ecclesiastical restriction whereby he was allowed to publish scientific but not religious works. (A distinction particularly difficult for Teilhard who considered God "the true object of science"; J,8/Mar/51.) In the following April he finished the essay explaining, "Intentionally I telescoped the question of the 'third reflection' (revelation) in a note" (Mortier, 30/Apr/52). The essay was published the following October without even the note (AE,321ff). Judging from the frequency of "R3" in his journals, it was a highly significant theme during the final years of his life. But aside from one article ("The Stuff of the Universe") the only published reference to revelation as third reflection would seem to be a cryptic and unexplained addendum to the text of a lecture: "Religious 'contact' = Initiation of the 3rd reflection (F^2/F^3) = neo-zest made explicit: Love (higher form of zest)" (AE,243).

5. This lack of soul in Humanity is symbolized several ways:

●	R1		$R1 = Vie^2a$		
	R2		$R2 = Vie^2b$		
	R3	J,2/July/51	$R3 = Vie^3$		J,20/July/52

In the set on the left R2 shows the elements harmoniously assembled, but they lack a center; they form a collective. In the set on the right the reflecting individual is considered Life squared, but Life is not cubed until R3.

6. That the movement from matter to spirit is identified with the movement from Object to Subject is implied in a set of drawings in Teilhard's Journal. He has an ellipse with foci identified as Object and Subject. This is identified as *Schema de Reflexion*. This is close to another ellipse with foci of matter and spirit and sets of arrows proceeding from the focus of matter to the focus of spirit (J,21,29/Oct/54).

7. Earlier in this chapter both the individual person and the earth-Noosphere

were presented as ellipses (see figure 3): each had a focus of complexity, a focus of the without identified as f_1 and F_1 respectively; and each had a focus of consciousness, a focus of the within identified as f_2 and F_2 respectively. The individual person was the Microcosm and the Noosphere was the Macrocosm. The growth in the individual's within deepens in parallel with the deepening of the Within of the Noosphere ("the growth of the 'within' only takes place thanks to a *double related involution,* the coiling up of the molecule on itself and the coiling up of the planet on itself" P,73). This could be correlated with the phases of reflection: An individual's conscious focus (f_2) is also his or her reflective soul (R_1); while the Noosphere's conscious focus (F_2) is not Humanity (R_2 in itself is without a focus), it is Christ (R_3). Thus, $R_3 = F_2 = \Omega =$ the term of matter's furling in on itself $=$ Christ $=$ the Revelation and Incarnation of God.

8. This is the point of several intricate passages: "I experienced unbelievable relief in feeling (*sentir*) that Another existed, and that through him all things existed, deep down within me" (W,123). The mystic "soon comes to see the world as no more than the back-wash (*remous*) of one essential Thing whose pleasure it is to react upon itself, within the conscious minds it supports," (W,125).

9. Perhaps some parallels in the religious tradition would help in understanding Teilhard: Kierkegaard would also locate God in a transposed human reflection: "he who loves God without faith reflects upon himself, he who loves God believingly reflects on God" (*Fear and Trembling,* 47). But Teilhard is best understood within the Platonic tradition. Plato tells a parable of prisoners in a cave; one prisoner is compelled "to turn his head around" (the "reversal"—he reflects); first he sees images and fire; then he makes an ascent "into the world of mind" (R_2) and above this sees the Sun, the Good (R_3). It was through reading the Platonists that St. Augustine resolved to turn within himself; this was the moment of his "conversion," his reversal. (Perhaps other references to conversion, repentance, and metanoia resemble Teilhard's reversal; the Kingdom of God is within. See HE,38.) Like Teilhard, Augustine found God to be an identity deeper than his own (*"intimior intimo meo"*); like Teilhard, Augustine would tell of God seeing the world through humanity's eyes ("It is you who see in us. Therefore, when we see that they (creatures) are good, you see they are good." Augustine, *Conf,*345); like Teilhard, Augustine would also tell of creation praising God through being known: "animals and material bodies praise you through the mouths of those who meditate upon them" Augustine, *Conf.* 90). There is a long tradition of spiritual writers who have spoken of the ascent of the mind to God; they saw all creation as a ladder or stairway of ascent. Teilhard belongs to this tradition. But for Teilhard this ladder is a sequence of scientific comprehensions. The ladder is still being created; each new hypothesis extends the creation.

Chapter 5

1. See Lukas, *Teilhard,* for a detailed account of Teilhard's many friendships with women.

2. For Teilhard the Feminine is closely allied with Matter; The Feminine is "dangerous life," and "dangerous force," and "the most formidable of the forces of matter"; it is "matter in its most virulent form" (J,284;T,74;T,66). Chastity is identified as "the climax of the problem of matter" (Li,263), and the problem of matter "in its acutest form," (LLZ,111).

3. Teilhard developed his thoughts on chastity during the First World War. In 1915 he urged that one not be hasty in dismissing the claim that the pursuit of an ideal proceeds from disordered sex (J,35). The sap of love is said to rise from sexual passion so that even the love of God is born of a transformation of sexual love (J,105–06). But he also told of the same reservation he would later have with full sexual expression: it "appears to neutralize the human monad"; it seems to neutralize rather than provide a new base of action (J,31,40).

4. Mlle. Jeanne Mortier, to whom Teilhard entrusted his manuscripts and who has directed their publication, told the present author that she received only a single text of the work. In 1926 Teilhard planned to write another version; what resulted was *The Divine Milieu,* a work that bears many traces of his first intention, e.g.: the Purity, Faith, & Fidelity treated are patterned on Offertory, Consecration, and Communion. In the summers of 1953 and 1954 he used the back pages of his Journal to outline new possibilities that would include the Gloria and Agnus Dei, etc. The same themes of growth and diminishment are present; the offertory is marked R2 and the consecration R3. He noted with enthusiasm the precise elements to be consecrated: the Flux of Convergence with its joys and pains, but this closely resembles the converging and Becoming in earlier versions. (W,208;HU,19,20).